Behind the Mask

THE LIFE OF QUEEN ELIZABETH I

By Jane Resh Thomas

Clarion Books / New York

ACKNOWLEDGMENTS

Thanks to the many people who have in various ways assisted me, especially Susan and Stephen Atkinson; Char and Martin White; Judy Spours and Oliver Kassmann; Jane, David, Susan, and Caroline Meacock; Pauline Soulsby; Major General Christopher Tyler C.B., then governor of the Tower of London, and Yeoman Warder Victor Lucas; Colonel Douglas McCord M.B.E., curator, and Robin Harcourt Williams, librarian of Hatfield House; assistant editor Jennifer Greene, and art director Anne Diebel. I am grateful to KTM (John Coy, Catherine Friend, Janet Lawson, Jody Peterson Lodge, Cindy Rogers, and Phyllis Root), and the Rainy Lake writers, who listened; Karen Ackerman, Dominick Cermele, Faith Finnberg, and Jason Thomas, who read; Richard Meacock, who advised and read, and Martin Stern, brothers and boon companions; and the Oberholtzer Foundation, which gave me the peace of Mallard Island while I worked on this book.

LIBRARY OF CONGRESS CATALOGING-IN-PUBLICATION DATA
Thomas, Jane Resh.
Behind the mask: the life of Queen Elizabeth I / by Jane Resh Thomas.
p.   cm.
Includes biographical references and index.
ISBN 0-395-69120-6
1. Elizabeth I, Queen of England, 1533–1603—Juvenile literature.   2. Great Britain—History—Elizabeth, 1533–1603—Juvenile literature.   3. Queens—Great Britain—Biography—Juvenile literature.   [1. Elizabeth I, Queen of England, 1533–1603.   2. Kings, queens, rulers, etc.   3. Women—Biography   4. Great Britain—History—Elizabeth, 1588–1603.]   I. Title.
DA355.T48   1998
942.05'5'092—dc20
[B]   94-31975
CIP   AC
CRW   10   9   8   7   6   5   4   3

To James Cross Giblin,
my editor, teacher, and friend,
and to Richard Meacock,
my English brother

CONTENTS

1. *Catherine of Aragon, a Spanish princess, Henry's first wife and the mother of Queen Mary I, was divorced to make way for Elizabeth's mother, Anne Boleyn.*

NATIONAL PORTRAIT GALLERY, LONDON.

6. *Katherine Parr, King Henry's sixth wife, survived him and remarried, but died after the birth of her only child.*

BY KIND PERMISSION OF HIS GRACE THE ARCHBISHOP OF CANTERBURY.

2. *Anne Boleyn, Elizabeth's mother, was beheaded by a swordsman before the princess's third birthday.*

NATIONAL PORTRAIT GALLERY, LONDON.

THE SIX WIVES OF HENRY VIII, FATHER OF ELIZABETH I

5. *The vivacious Katherine Howard, a cousin of Anne Boleyn, was beheaded for adultery.*

BY KIND PERMISSION OF HER MAJESTY QUEEN ELIZABETH II.

4. *Henry's distaste for his fourth wife, Anne of Cleves, helped bring about the execution of the official who had urged the marriage.*

MUSÉE DU LOUVRE, PARIS.

3. *Jane Seymour, mother of King Edward VI, died of a massive infection after childbirth.*

KUNSTHISTORISCHES MUSEUM, VIENNA

CAST OF CHARACTERS

Henry Tudor 1491–1547

King Henry VIII of England 1509–1547, second son of King Henry VII. Inherited the throne after his elder brother and then his father died.

HENRY'S WIVES

1. Catherine* of Aragon 1485–1536

Daughter of King Ferdinand and Queen Isabella of Spain. Wife of Henry VIII 1509–1533; mother of Mary Tudor. Marriage of Catherine and Henry annulled after his secret marriage to Anne Boleyn.

2. Anne Boleyn 1507?–1536

Daughter of a knight, niece of Duke of Norfolk, and relative of the noble Howard family. Maid of honor to Catherine of Aragon. Wife of Henry VIII 1533–1536; gave birth to Elizabeth Tudor 1533. Convicted of adultery and incest, beheaded for treason.

3. Jane Seymour 1509?–1537

Maid of honor to Catherine of Aragon and Anne Boleyn. Became Henry's wife in 1536, less than two weeks after Anne's execution. Gave birth to Edward Tudor 1537, died of infection ("childbed fever") twelve days later.

4. Anne of Cleves 1515–1557

German Protestant princess. Henry married her in January 1540, divorced her in July.

*The given names of Catherine of Aragon, Katherine Howard, and Katherine Parr vary in spelling, beginning sometimes with the letter *C* and sometimes *K*. For the sake of clarity, these spellings are used throughout the book.

5. **Katherine Howard** 1521–1542

Niece of powerful Duke of Norfolk, and cousin of Anne Boleyn. Became Henry's wife soon after his divorce from Anne of Cleves. Charged with adultery late the following year. Beheaded for treason.

6. **Katherine Parr** 1512–1548

Rich daughter of court official. Married Henry VIII 1543. After his death in 1547 married Thomas Seymour, brother of Jane Seymour, Henry's deceased third wife. Died of childbed fever following year.

HENRY'S CHILDREN

Mary Tudor 1516–1558

Queen Mary I of England 1553–1558. Only surviving child of Henry VIII and his first wife, Catherine of Aragon.

Elizabeth Tudor 1533–1603

Queen Elizabeth I of England 1558–1603. Only surviving child of Henry VIII and his second wife, Anne Boleyn.

Edward Tudor 1537–1553

King Edward VI of England 1547–1553. Only child of Henry VIII and his third wife, Jane Seymour.

CONTENDERS FOR THE ENGLISH THRONE

Jane Grey 1537–1554

Queen of England for nine days 1553. Granddaughter of King Henry VIII's younger sister, Mary. Protector John Dudley forced her marriage to his son Guilford, declared her queen in order to usurp the throne after Edward VI died. Beheaded.

Mary Stuart 1542–1587

Queen of Scots 1542–1567, Queen of France 1559–1560. Only child of James V of Scotland and Mary of Guise. Granddaughter of Margaret, elder sister of Henry VIII. Wife of King Francis II of France, then of Henry Stuart, Lord Darnley, then of the Earl of Bothwell.

James Stuart 1566–1625

King James VI of Scotland 1567–1625, King James I of England 1603–1625, after Elizabeth I. Son of Mary, Queen of Scots, and Henry Stuart, Lord Darnley.

OTHER ROYALTY

Charles 1500–1558

King Charles I of Spain 1516–1556, Hapsburg Holy Roman Emperor Charles V 1519–1558. Grandson of Queen Isabella and King Ferdinand, nephew of Catherine of Aragon, father of King Philip II of Spain.

Francis II 1544–1560

King Francis II of France 1559–1560. First husband of Mary, Queen of Scots.

Francis 1554–1584

French prince, Duke of Alençon and Anjou. Suitor of Elizabeth I (her Frog), youngest brother of Kings Francis II, Charles IX, and Henry III of France.

Philip 1527–1598

King Philip II of Spain 1556–1598. Son of Emperor Charles V, husband of Queen Mary I of England 1554. In 1588 launched Spanish Armada, which the English devastated.

COURTIERS

William Cecil, Lord Burghley 1520–1598

Secretary of state to Elizabeth I 1558–1572, lord treasurer 1572–1598.

Robert Cecil, Earl of Salisbury 1563–1612

Secretary of state to Elizabeth, unofficially from about 1589, formally from 1596 until her death. Organized succession of James I and continued to serve him.

Robert Devereux, Earl of Essex 1567–1601

Stepson of Robert Dudley. Favorite of Elizabeth I. Planned a coup against her government. Beheaded for treason.

John Dudley, Duke of Northumberland 1502?–1553

Protector of England during reign of King Edward VI, having deposed Edward Seymour, Duke of Somerset. Persuaded King Edward VI to disinherit his half-sisters, Mary and Elizabeth. Engineered proclamation of Jane Grey as queen. Beheaded for treason.

Robert Dudley, Earl of Leicester (Robin) 1532?–1588

Intimate friend, master of the horse, and privy councilor to Elizabeth I. Queen's favorite, but reputation permanently damaged when his wife, Amy Robsart, died mysteriously. Patron of literature, especially drama. Military leader during attack of Spanish Armada in 1588.

Edward Seymour, Duke of Somerset 1506?–1552

Brother of Jane Seymour, third wife of Henry VIII. Protector of England during reign of his nephew, King Edward VI. Removed from office by councilors led by John Dudley, and beheaded.

Thomas Seymour 1508?–1549

Brother of Jane Seymour; husband of dowager queen, Katherine Parr, surviving wife of Henry VIII. Lord admiral during reign of his nephew, King Edward VI. Suitor of Princess Elizabeth. Beheaded for treason by protector government of his brother, Edward Seymour.

Henry Stuart, Lord Darnley 1545–1567

Grandson of Margaret Tudor, sister of Henry VIII. Second husband of Mary, Queen of Scots. Murdered mysteriously, perhaps with approval of his wife.

Sir Francis Walsingham 1532?–1590

Secretary of state to Elizabeth I from 1573 until his death. Militant Protestant; developed extensive spy network that entrapped Mary, Queen of Scots.

Thomas Wolsey 1473?–1530

Privy (private) councilor of Henry VIII, administered government, nearly controlled domestic and foreign policy 1514–1529. Cardinal of Roman Catholic Church. Ruined by failure to procure annulment of Henry's marriage to Catherine of Aragon and enable the king's marriage to Anne Boleyn. Died while traveling to trial for treason.

Thomas Wyatt ?–1554

Raised small army against Queen Mary I when she decided to marry the Catholic Philip of Spain. Exonerated Princess Elizabeth from involvement in plot; hanged for treason.

A sober Princess Elizabeth in adolescence, dressed relatively plainly, at a time when clothing could suggest allegiance to one religion or another. By kind permission of Her Majesty Queen Elizabeth II.

1
THE MIDNIGHT CROW

THE FIRST ELIZABETH OF ENGLAND, who died not quite four hundred years ago, became such a great queen that she gave her name to her time, the Elizabethan Age. She impressed herself more vividly on the memory of the world than any other monarch in English history. Eventually she won the personal respect of both enemies and friends, and she led England at the dawn of its influence as a great nation. She protected her country from being swallowed by its greedy neighbors or consumed by civil war. Despite hostility to her gender, she established and maintained her power, carved a career and a life of her own, and refused to subject herself to men.

Yet Elizabeth is wrapped and mummified in myths and fantasies that make it difficult for one to see her as a whole human being. Princesses, everyone supposes, lead enchanted lives. They are born into splendor and power. Their subjects grant their every wish. Beloved by the kingdom; dressed by servants in jewels and gold, silk and velvet; pampered and treasured by kings and married to princes— they seem to have everything.

But the real life of Elizabeth shows how false such fantasies may be. If she was charmed, then her enchanter must have been an evil fairy whose charm was at least in part a curse. For many of Elizabeth's subjects despised her from her infancy. Her father put her mother to death and neglected Elizabeth for much of her childhood. Wealthy though she was, money constantly worried her, for her personal fortune, derived from her lands and investments, was not always enough to support the government, the army and navy, and her several enormous households. And although she found a prince she called her "Frog," she never found one she could love.

The official myths that Elizabeth encouraged about herself are as misleading as our own fantasies. Appealing though these images may be, they are only half true. According to one of them, she was Good Queen Bess. She does seem to have understood the plight of the common people with remarkable compassion. She loved them and won the loyalty even of subjects who deeply disagreed with her. She could be ruthless, however, a monarch whose principles of government resembled those of Machiavelli, the Italian political writer whose book, *The Prince*, she could have read. He advised rulers to consider their own power and self-interest above all else and argued that lies and deceit, cruelty and violence, were acceptable means of gaining and keeping power. London Bridge and the gates of the city often bore the heads and carcasses of Elizabeth's executed subjects during her reign.

The myth of Gloriana makes Elizabeth a goddess wrapped in embroidered silk, woven gold, and ropes of pearls, bestriding the world. In her portraits she looks like a stuffed doll, impossibly grand, a creature above flaws and doubt. But her government dictated the patterns of her portraits and censored all other images. Doubt hounded her, but she hid it, like her mistakes, to survive. If she had shown any weakness, her enemies would have attacked. Despite her official grandeur, she swore at her courtiers and threw tantrums and shocked her visitors. And she enjoyed fights staged between bears and dogs as much as she did Shakespeare's plays.

Elizabeth also encouraged the myth of the Virgin Queen. It is true that she never married. She knew that, if she did, she would lose her power to her husband and thereby hand over England either to one of her own subjects or to a foreign prince. But throughout Europe, people gossiped that she was sexually promiscuous. We can never know, but there is reason to think that she may have had lovers.

Yet for all the half-truths, for all her faults, Elizabeth left her unique handprint on the history of the world. Owing partly to skill and intelligence and partly to luck, she lived just short of seventy years and reigned for nearly forty-five. Her long life can rightly be called a feat, because Elizabeth was threatened with murder from the day she was born a princess to the day she died a queen. She suffered imprisonment, death threats from her half-sister, and attempts to force her to marry men she despised. Her friends mounted rebellion in her name, thereby implicating her in treason and risking her life. Her enemies plotted rebellion against her, scheming to shoot, stab, or poison her.

Elizabeth's life was a curious mixture of luxury and pain, for she wore her rubies and pearls, her velvet and silk, at a time when bubonic plague and other diseases killed multitudes, royalty and commoners alike. It was a time when even palaces were drafty, flea-ridden mansions heated only by open fires. The best roads were mere tracks in the dirt, and to maintain them every householder was required to labor several days each year or send a substitute. Nobody dreamed of freedom or self-governance for anyone but kings and popes, and even they were hemmed in by tradition, religion, politics, and a shortage of money.

Royalty experienced the same physical discomforts and illness as everybody else. In addition, Elizabeth was born to the Tudors, a very unhappy royal family. A striking difference between ordinary family problems and those of the Tudors was that, when the king was unhappy, he could blame other people and order their executions.

King Henry VIII, painted in 1536, when he was beginning to lose the vigor and handsome looks of his youth. Elizabeth's mother, Anne Boleyn, was executed that same year, before the princess was three years old. NATIONAL PORTRAIT GALLERY, LONDON.

The peril to the princess began before her birth, for she was born into a scorpion's nest. When he was nineteen years old, her father, King Henry VIII, had married his brother's widow, Catherine of Aragon. Such a marriage between a man and his sister-in-law required the special permission of the pope. Six years older than Henry, Catherine was a proud Spanish princess, the daughter of King Ferdinand and Queen Isabella of Spain, the monarchs who had financed the voyage of Columbus to America. Like Henry and nearly everybody else in England, Catherine was a pious Christian who believed wholeheartedly in the teachings of the Roman Catholic Church.

Royal marriages were rarely love matches, however. Instead, they served two great national purposes. If carefully planned, they created alliances between political factions or between nations to consolidate the power of the crown. Equally important, a king's marriage produced the child who would inherit his realm. In England the king's eldest son stood first among the heirs to the throne, the line of succession. Next came his brothers, in order of age, unless the heir had produced sons of his own. There was always great pressure on the king or his eldest son to produce a male heir.

Henry's marriage to Catherine had formed an alliance between England and Spain against France, but she had failed in her duty to produce a male heir to the throne. (People of that time did not know that it is the father's sperm cell that determines the gender of the child.) Although Catherine had given birth to at least six children, only one daughter, Mary, born in 1516, survived.

Henry did have two sons, but they were the children of mistresses, Elizabeth Blount and Mary Boleyn, who had been Catherine's maids of honor. Elizabeth Blount's son, Henry Fitzroy, the Earl of Richmond, was a respected presence in the court. (At the age of six he was served meals that cost as much as a farmer earned in twenty months.) Mary Boleyn's child is a mysterious figure who has disappeared from history.

Since these sons were illegitimate, not the children of Henry's legal wife, their claim to the throne was doubtful at best. But their existence proved to Henry that the lack of a legitimate male heir was Catherine's problem, not his. The fact that Catherine had not given birth to a boy, the king said, showed that God disapproved of his marriage to his widowed sister-in-law. It was Henry's duty to the realm, he declared, to father a son. Doing so, he would secure the throne and prevent the civil war that would surely follow his death if the succession came to a fight. Henry began scheming to annul his marriage to Catherine, as if it had never happened. And if the marriage did not exist, then Catherine and Henry's daughter Mary was illegitimate, with no right to the throne.

What Henry did not admit was his passion for yet another maid of honor, Anne Boleyn, a woman who had grown up at the French court. France's ambassador reported to his government that Henry's infatuation was so wild, only God could relieve his madness. The opposite of the prim and aging Catherine, Anne was a vivacious flirt, a sensual magnet to men, high-spirited and temperamental, with black hair, black eyes, and a very long neck.

Anne Boleyn, the mother of Elizabeth and second wife of Henry VIII, after her marriage. Her portrait shows the long neck and large "goggle" eyes for which she was noted, but none of the deformities reported years after her death by people who never saw her. NATIONAL PORTRAIT GALLERY, LONDON.

For years she resisted an affair with Henry, not wishing to be, like her sister Mary, the outcast mother of the king's bastard child. Anne Boleyn insisted on marriage. Her aloofness may have been attractive, but she was also arrogant and tactless. As Henry courted her, she dressed her servants in clothing embroidered with the motto "Let them grumble, that is how it is going to be," written in French. Haughty, depending upon her favor with the king, she did not try to make other powerful friends. She loved a little lapdog named Purkoy so much, and was so shrill with her servants, they were afraid to tell her when it died in a fall.

Though Henry had courted other women, Queen Catherine had never lost her official place. Now he demanded that she give up her jewels so that Anne might wear them when she traveled to France with him. Catherine turned over her jewelry, but she would not give up her title of wife.

Thomas Cardinal Wolsey, the top servant in King Henry's government, was also a high official in the Roman Catholic Church. He hated Anne, whom he called the Midnight Crow, for the trouble she had stirred. Nevertheless, Wolsey tried to persuade the pope, leader of the Church, to dissolve Henry's marriage to Catherine. Although the Church in principle opposed divorce, a pope could adapt the law for royalty as he saw fit; he might even permit a king who had no sons to marry a second wife. When Catherine persisted in her stubborn refusal to renounce her marriage to Henry, however, she put the pope in a political pinch.

Catherine's nephew was the Hapsburg Holy Roman Emperor Charles V, who was king of Spain as well, the most powerful man in Europe. He had recently sacked Rome, the home of the Catholic Church. If the pope dissolved Catherine's marriage, Charles might take revenge and attack him again with the Hapsburg army. This risk the pope could not take.

On the other hand, King Henry threatened to sever the tie between the English Church and Rome if his wishes were denied. Apart from its duty to preserve Christianity, the Church could not afford such a loss of money and power. The choices Henry had forced on the pope were both so obnoxious that the church's leader was seen weeping as he contemplated them.

Power during King Henry's reign was divided. Roman Catholicism was the official church in Christian Europe. Membership was required of everybody. Catholics paid a fixed amount of their income to the Church, and part of that money went to Rome. Throughout Europe a pope was the highest authority, the religious equivalent of king. The pope ruled the Church and the spiritual life of the people, including kings and emperors, as a monarch ruled the realm and his subjects' bodily lives.

The king could decide what his people's religion ought to be, but a pope could destroy a king's power. People who disobeyed the pope's moral commands were punished by excommunication. This expulsion from the Church meant the loss of one's place in the community, and an excommunicated soul could not reach Heaven.

This time King Henry and the pope clashed head-on, and neither would budge. Cardinal Wolsey, charged in 1530 with high treason for failing his mission, died on the way to trial. Henry had waited for years while Wolsey tried to dissolve the king's marriage by persuasion. Now the king committed an amazing act of defiance. He declared himself the head of the English Church, subject only to God. He bullied the clergy, who dutifully ruled his marriage to Catherine illegal. She was sent to a remote house in the country on the edge of the Fens. So few people lived in this gigantic marsh that her residence there was like imprisonment. The king's agents watched to prevent her escape to Spain.

Eventually Henry would disband the Catholic Church's monasteries, seizing their immense treasure and lands to enrich himself and his friends; their gratitude to him reinforced his political power. The religious strife that resulted from this break with the Church rocked England for a hundred years, but Henry was happy. In a private ceremony during late 1532 or early 1533, witnessed only by the bride's parents, her brother, and two friends, Henry married Anne Boleyn. She had given in to passion and was probably pregnant before the wedding.

Despite the disruption of their religious life, King Henry's people went along with him. They had been Catholics for centuries, but the religious discontent that disturbed all of Europe troubled England too. A corrupt priesthood had made the English cynical. This corruption took several forms. Some of it was greed and extravagance—the gold plates, pearl headdresses, and palaces that the princes of the Church enjoyed while others starved. Some of the wrongs were sexual—priests lived openly with prostitutes.

These were sins on an individual scale, but great authorities committed greater injuries. Corrupt Church officials exploited the people for money. The Bishop of Winchester controlled Southwark, a suburb across the river from London that was a haven for criminals. Most people who committed felonies were executed. Criminals were hanged and their bodies cut into quarters in St. Paul's churchyard. Yet indirectly crime had made the bishop rich. This same clergy who benefited from sin had tortured and killed multitudes accused of sin. Many people therefore felt contempt for priests, feared them, and even hated them.

In Continental Europe, across the Channel from England, Martin Luther and some other Protestants agitated for religious freedom. What they wanted, though, was a simpler creed stripped of ornate vestments, decorations, and rituals, freedom to practice *their* religion . . . and to force everybody else to do the same. Henry did not join the Protestants against the power of the Church. Indeed, he wrote a book attacking Luther's rebellion against authority. Henry merely wanted that power and authority for himself. And though the people were alarmed, they did not stand openly with the pope against the king.

The streets of London were a crowded open market, where people bought and sold everything from turnips, coal, and wool to monkeys and peacocks. While Henry could control the clergy with threats, not all the people on the streets would obey gladly. Sometimes a rebellious bystander called out an insult and then faded into the mob without punishment. Many faithful Catholics who had loved Queen Catherine resented King Henry's annulment of his marriage. When he married Anne Boleyn and appeared publicly with her, some people pointed at the flags decorated with the intertwined initials of the royal names, *H* and *A*, and hooted, "HA HA!" Grumble as the people might, however, as Anne said, things were as they were going to be.

When Anne became pregnant, the court astrologer (the nearest thing to a scientist in England) and doctors told Henry what he wanted to hear. The baby would certainly be a boy, they said. Catherine had received an exquisite robe from Spain for the christening of her babies. Henry commanded her to turn over this christening robe to Anne. Catherine refused, and the royal needlewomen embroidered a new one.

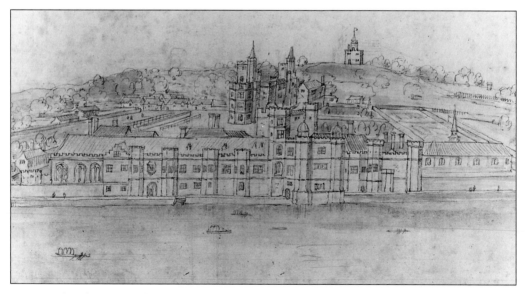

Greenwich Palace, on the banks of the River Thames, where both Elizabeth and her father were born. ASHMOLEAN MUSEUM.

A magnificent bed that had once ransomed a captured French nobleman was brought from the royal treasury for the birth of Anne's child. Workmen took it by boat to Greenwich, the royal palace where King Henry himself had been born. A letter was written to announce that God had blessed the people by "bringing forth a prince." The king's men planned a great jousting tournament to celebrate the arrival of the heir to Henry's throne. Despite all the royal expectations, the baby born September 7, 1533, was a girl: a perfect and beautiful girl, but nevertheless a girl. The word *prince* on the royal announcement had to be changed to *princess.*

The severity of Henry's disappointment with the birth of Elizabeth makes sense only in light of his ideas. He and other people in his time believed in a God-designed hierarchy, a ladder of value with God at the top and the king and pope just below him, representing God on earth. Mammals were superior to fish, which were superior to worms. Since human beings were placed by God's law above all other creatures, humanity properly ruled the animals. Similarly, people assumed that men were naturally superior to women, and women to children.

These ideas of hierarchy were expressed in the laws, including the law of inheritance. It was eldest sons, not daughters, who succeeded their fathers to the throne; according to the beliefs of the time, only a male could govern well. If a woman was the sole heir to the throne, without brothers, her supposed weakness of intelligence and moral frailty were seen as disastrous to the realm. In the recent past, England had suffered terrible wars to decide who would be king. The country needed an heir to Henry's throne whose right to it would not be questioned.

When the child born to Anne was a daughter, it seemed that God had once again thwarted the king's hope of fathering a male heir. Anne's enemies, who called her "the goggle-eyed whore," now named the infant "the little whore." Some said that she was not the king's child at all but a serving woman's baby. The church bells rang out in celebration, though, and the people of London lit bon-fires and drank barrels of the king's wine. A foreign ambassador sarcastically said that they were celebrating King Henry's disappointment. Henry had decided to name his second daughter Mary, like his first, but changed his mind at the last moment. He canceled the tournament, and he did not attend the christening ceremony at which the newborn child, in memory of his mother, was named Elizabeth.

2
SISTERS

DESPITE HENRY'S DISAPPOINTMENT at the birth of a daughter instead of the son he wanted, the baby was christened in an elaborate ceremony befitting a princess. She wore a purple velvet mantle. In a chapel perfumed with incense and decorated with storytelling tapestries and bright handmade rugs, she was undressed behind a curtain, warmed by coals that glowed in an iron container.

The Bishop of London dipped the back of her head and her heels in holy water, touched her chest and her back with the holy oil that only royalty had a right to, and named her Elizabeth. Ten months later, when the pope excommunicated her father, two priests would declare in a sermon that Elizabeth had been christened in hot water, but not hot enough.

The princess was given two cradles. One was carved wood that had been painted gold. The other was upholstered in crimson cloth of gold, a fabric made of red silk threads woven across finely spun metallic gold threads, with a coverlet lined in ermine, the finest white fur.

When Elizabeth grew a little older, Anne ordered dresses made especially for the child by the royal seamstresses, in white damask, green satin, and yellow silk; white and green were the Tudor colors. Sleeves were not attached to anybody's clothing then, but were tied or pinned in place. Elizabeth had embroidered sleeves made of crimson, white, and purple velvet. Her coats were russet, black, and orange, which must have emphasized her handsome dark eyes and red-gold hair. Her purple caps were trimmed with gold. Growing up as the daughter of King Henry, the most powerful person in the realm, Elizabeth seems to have had the best of everything.

Henry had been a charming golden-haired giant in his youth, six feet three or four inches tall, taller than all his courtiers but one. He loved hunting and jousting, but he was also a learned man who hired fine musicians for his entertainment. He even composed some songs himself, a few of which survive.

Unlike his father, who was stingy because he knew that the realm's strength depended upon a strong economy, Henry spent extravagantly on magnificent palaces and pleasure. He ate the richest foods from gold and silver dishes. He dressed in furs and silk. His gardens were planted with strange new specimens brought from distant lands. Henry also invested in military projects. He had the foresight to build a powerful navy to protect his island kingdom from attack by France and Spain, the strongest nations of Europe. During his reign England began to challenge their power.

The king and his court were magnificent. But writers in Henry's England often expressed the idea that appearances are not the same as reality; a terrible rot may underlie a bright surface. As Shakespeare later put it, "All that glisters [glitters] is not gold." So it was with King Henry. Indeed, his daughters did have the best of everything, except a peaceful family.

When Elizabeth was born, Henry was forty-two years old—which was considered aged in those times. He was still dashing, not yet the grotesquely fat and swollen figure that his bottomless stomach would make him before ten years had passed. But his health was declining. Because of a painful ulcer on his thigh that would not heal, he needed to use a gold walking stick. He slept poorly and suffered frequent sore throats and headaches. Now that Wolsey no longer helped run the government, the responsibility weighed on the king. He was short-tempered and unscrupulous.

The moment Elizabeth was born, a herald in the next room announced that Henry and Catherine's only daughter, the seventeen-year-old Mary, was no longer Princess of Wales (the title always borne by the heir to the throne). Her insignias were removed from the clothing of her servants and replaced with the king's, as if to show who owned these people—indeed who owned Mary herself. And now the king was displaying his naked new baby to ambassadors at court, to prove that she was normal, a fit prospect for marriage. Suddenly Elizabeth had taken the place of her half-sister in both the marriage market and her father's affection.

Her parents' battle had burdened Mary since the age of eleven. When their marriage had at last been nullified, Mary's own position changed utterly. She had once been the darling of the court, whose betrothal to the future King of France was celebrated with pomp and dancing. Though Mary did not accompany Catherine to the Fens, the former heir to the throne had practically ceased to exist, and the two outcasts were not allowed to comfort one another; after Catherine's banishment, Henry never permitted Mary and her mother to meet again. Now considered a bastard, the child of an unmarried mother, Mary had been reduced from princess to mere lady, and the newborn baby was heir to the throne.

The story of Mary's loss of status is like a fairy tale about a princess rejected by her father and her wicked stepmother. Mary was one of the people who could

Mary Tudor, Elizabeth's half-sister and daughter of Catherine of Aragon, in 1554, soon after her accession to the throne as Mary I, Queen of England. NATIONAL PORTRAIT GALLERY, LONDON.

not forgive the destruction of Catherine, but she blamed the annulment on her father's new wife. Anne had said that she would make Catherine of Aragon and Mary her serving women. As soon as Anne became queen, she set about humiliating the rival to her own and Elizabeth's power.

Mary was required to be present at Elizabeth's birth. Her household was dissolved, her 160 servants dismissed. At the age of three months, the baby was sent away from her parents to a household of her own at Hatfield Royal Palace. Mary went with her, demoted to the status of servant, the newborn princess's maid of honor. Elizabeth traveled with great ceremony and splendor to demonstrate to the people of London that the power had shifted and the order of succession to the throne had changed.

All marks of Mary's former rank were snatched away, and Anne directed the servants to strike the young woman's ears and slap her "for being the cursed bastard she is." At dinner she no longer sat in her accustomed place under the canopy of state, an overhead swath of beautiful cloth that honored royalty. Now the lady Mary dined far down the table from Princess Elizabeth, out of the way. Refusing to accept the insult, she tried to eat alone in her own rooms, the most unpleasant apartment in the palace. Anne ordered her to return to the common dining hall and accept her new place at the table.

Mary also refused to address her baby sister as the Princess of Wales, saying, "That is a title which belongs to me by right, and to no one else." On journeys, Elizabeth rode in a velvet litter carried by servants. (There were no carriages or coaches in England until the 1550s. One was built for Elizabeth in 1564.) When Mary refused to take second place, men dragged her away from the litter and forced her to sit in a plain conveyance with the gentlewomen.

Once Mary asked to ride horseback when the household was moving, as it often did, so that the palace could be cleaned. Granted permission, she dashed away on her horse and arrived at the royal barge on the river long before the others. By the time the little Elizabeth arrived, Mary had taken the seat of honor and refused to move.

All the people in the realm were the king's servants, his children among them, but Mary opposed her father as fiercely as her mother had. Mary's disgrace affected not only protocol and precedence, but her personal safety. The year after Elizabeth's birth, Henry's government passed a law that formally transferred to Anne's children the right to inherit the throne. If Henry should die now, Anne would be regent, governing for her children until they grew to adulthood; she would likely execute both Catherine and her daughter to eliminate their claim to power. Mary became seriously ill, but no doctor would treat her for fear of being held responsible in case Anne had poisoned Mary. Servants said aloud that they hoped she would die.

Henry commanded the devoutly Catholic Mary publicly to renounce her religion as well as her parents' marriage. When she refused, the king sent Thomas Howard, Duke of Norfolk, Anne's uncle, to force Mary's cooperation. She still refused. Norfolk shouted that if she were his own daughter, he would beat her to death. He would smash her head against the wall until it was "soft as a boiled apple." Mary faced down the enraged courtier, standing as tall as a small woman could, and declared again in her rough, low voice that she was forever a faithful Catholic and the daughter of the king's legal wife.

When Norfolk returned to court, Henry said that the duke had been too easy on Mary. If she should call herself *princess* or her mother *queen* even once, she was told, she would be sent to the Tower of London, a great stone castle that served also as the government's armory and prison. Threatened by her own father with life imprisonment or even death if she refused, Mary at last took the oath of loyalty to Anne and her children.

Now Henry was in effect pope of England as well as its king, a change that sanctioned his desires as the will of God. The Protestant leader Martin Luther remarked with scorn, "Squire Henry wishes to be God and to do as he pleases." Although religious doctrine continued unchanged, the pope's authority was enormously damaged throughout Europe. The English Church no longer obeyed the pope's orders, but answered only to the king; it would pay no more money to the central Church in Rome, nor would such questions about religious law as whether the king's marriage was valid be decided there.

In retaliation, the pope took the drastic step of excommunicating Henry. This act automatically deposed him from his throne, relieved his subjects of the obligation to obey him, and threatened the realm with war. Rebellion was in the air, and the Catholics in the north of England were on the brink of armed resistance. Four monks who refused to accept the king as Supreme Head of the Church in England were hanged, castrated, and disemboweled, their organs pulled from their bellies while they were still alive. Even Thomas More, the great Catholic author of *Utopia*, a book about the ideal state, was not immune. Henry imprisoned and, in 1535, beheaded his old friend and adviser for refusing to take the Supremacy Oath.

Mary signed the papers that declared her parents' marriage illegal. She also acknowledged her father as Supreme Head of the Church of England, but she defiantly practiced traditional Catholicism until she died. Nevertheless, she always felt guilty about her betrayal of both her mother and her religion. Having bullied her to renounce them both, Henry took Mary back as his beloved child, but she had lost to the upstarts, Anne and her little daughter, almost everything that mattered. Circumstances more likely to cause antagonism between sisters can hardly be imagined.

On the day of Catherine's death, January 8, 1536, Henry and Anne celebrated. There had always been a risk that Emperor Charles V would invade England to rescue Catherine of Aragon and punish the king's cruelty to Catherine and her daughter. That threat had now ended. Henry and Anne and Elizabeth wore yellow silk, the color of rejoicing, and the king swept up the two-year-old princess in his arms, dancing her from room to room. "Praised be God, who has freed us from all suspicion of war," he cried.

Happiness in the royal palace never lasted for long, however. On the day that Catherine was buried, Anne gave birth prematurely to a baby, apparently a male, who died.

The contrast was extreme between the sharp-tongued Anne and the dignified Catherine, who had accepted whatever Henry did until he dissolved his sacred marriage vows to her. His affairs with other women resumed, now that Anne had married him. When she upbraided him about his lovers, he told her that she must shut her eyes and endure, as others who were better than she had done before. She ought to know that he could lower her at any time as much as he had raised her.

Any spirited woman married to such a king would have been in danger. Anne dressed extravagantly and, as a Protestant, tried to lecture Henry on religion. Accustomed to lecturing others on that subject, he was furious. She treated his friends and the officers of his government with contempt and made enemies everywhere. Her own relatives both feared and scorned her. When her second baby died, the king began to wonder whether this marriage was the one God wanted for him. And when she lost a third baby, a boy, early in the pregnancy, a courtier remarked that she had "miscarried of her savior."

At that time, childbirth was seen as a queen's duty; any wife of Henry's was barren at her peril. If she failed in childbearing, her principal role in life, she was deemed not only inadequate but even unnatural. Henry felt that God had cursed his marriage to Anne—the death of her babies proved it. As he often did, he was using God as an excuse for his own desires. Henry had become infatuated with another young woman, Jane Seymour. Ironically, she was Anne's maid of honor, as Anne had once been Catherine's. Henry hoped that a new wife would give him a boy.

When Elizabeth was two years and eight months old, her mother was walking with her in the royal gardens at Greenwich Palace. Seeing the king in the window above, Queen Anne lifted Elizabeth in her arms and displayed her, trying to pacify him with their child. Henry looked down coldly, as if Elizabeth and her mother were invisible. Three days later his soldiers arrested Anne and took her to the Tower. Her enemies had plotted a way to bring her down and free the king of a wife who was not only bad-tempered but barren, except for her useless daughter.

Anne was tried for adultery with five men, including her brother. All but one proclaimed Anne innocent until they died, and the confession of that one was forced. He had been tortured on the rack, a device that stretched the human body

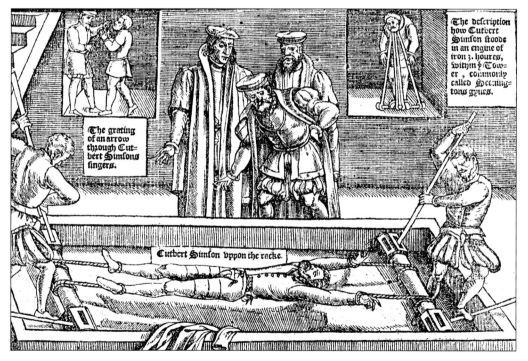

A man being stretched on the rack, an implement of torture legally used in Tudor England to force confessions. Two inset pictures above show other means of torture. BRITISH LIBRARY.

until the joints tore apart. (Both religious and governmental authorities considered torture a legal and proper act in cases of high treason.) The tribunal that heard Anne's case included Norfolk, her uncle; saying he was ill, her father was excused. All the members of the tribunal owed their position in society to Henry and were at his mercy. They found Anne guilty of high treason, for which a queen's punishment was either beheading or burning at the stake.

The true story will never be known, for we have only the records of Henry's government and its charges against Anne; Henry's servants were quite willing to trump up a case. It is not credible, however, that such an intelligent, worldly woman as Anne Boleyn, who had been brought up amid the intrigues at the French court, would take such a risk as adultery. The woman who had held off the amorous king for six years, refusing a sexual liaison with him while he was married, is not likely to have thrown away her crown and her life for fleeting affairs. On some of the dates of the alleged adultery, Anne was in different places from the ones alleged. Moreover, she was a committed Christian who, like her contemporaries, believed in a literal hell; and she swore her innocence just before she died, even as she took the sacrament.

One historian, Retha M. Warnicke, speculates that Anne's third child may have been born deformed, a circumstance typically blamed on witchcraft and intercourse with the devil. The mighty King Henry seems to have implied at Anne's trial that he was impotent: she had bewitched him, he claimed, making him incapable of fatherhood at the time the child was conceived. He might have done so to avoid association with her infant's deformity.

There are other peculiarities in the biographies of Anne. Decades after her death, a writer who had never seen her described an extra finger on one hand and a black birthmark on her neck, and biographers ever since have picked up this legend as if it were factual. But why would a king, so concerned about his heirs, marry a woman with such obvious deformities? The writer was a fervid

Catholic eager to attribute satanic characteristics to the woman who had indirectly caused the English Reformation. Nobody who knew Anne ever mentioned these traits.

The factual questions suggest the difficulty of knowing the truth centuries after events. Records are incomplete. Bias of witnesses is difficult to assess. Destruction of evidence counter to a government's case is impossible to discover. The fact is that the only story we have about Anne is the one cooked up by Henry's officials. And the tribunal found her guilty.

While she waited in her Tower room, a fine French swordsman sailed across the English Channel from Calais. The hiring of his services was taken as a kindness, a quick death for Anne rather than the prolonged agony of burning or the clumsy butchery of the axe. But first, two days after the verdict, she was forced to watch the deaths of her brother and the other men accused with her. Two bodies were dismembered; the scaffold was awash with blood.

On a fine May morning two days later, wearing an ermine mantle, a loose gray gown, and a crimson petticoat, the queen whose servants had worn the motto "The Most Happy" embroidered in French on their clothing was taken by her guards to the green at the Tower of London. As the king's bastard son, Henry Fitzroy, and other noblemen watched, Anne knelt upright. The executioner from Calais had hidden his weapon in the straw that was strewn around the platform. He called, "Bring me a sword!" to someone who stood on the steps. Anne turned toward the assistant. While she was distracted, the swordsman suddenly cut off her head with one stroke of his sharp blade. The force caused her head to roll some distance.

Anne's head and her body were wrapped in separate sheets and placed in a crude elm storage chest made for bows and arrows, because the king and his agents had forgotten to order a proper coffin. The guardsmen buried her without a religious service under the altar in the Tower church, St. Peter in Chains.

As his wife went to her death, the king was off a-hunting. Within eleven days he was betrothed to marry the submissive Jane Seymour. Though Henry put his wives behind him without looking back, others have not forgotten Anne. Even now, every May 19, an unknown party sends a bouquet to her grave.

Nobody remembers where Elizabeth was during Anne's trial and death, or how she learned of the loss. But everyone in the kingdom soon knew that the little princess, not yet three years old, was now a motherless child.

3
THE MIDNIGHT CROW'S DAUGHTER

ELIZABETH MAY NOT HAVE KNOWN HER MOTHER well enough to miss her greatly when she died, for servants had tended the princess from the day she was born. Queens and other highborn women were considered above changing their children's diapers, guiding them, disciplining them. Anne had provided the child with fine clothing, but she had never cared for her physical needs. The women who breast-fed Elizabeth and kept her clean, who rocked her and put her to bed, were still with her. Whatever turmoil occurred around Elizabeth, even the death of her mother, the circle of people who loved her and tended her every day remained stable. She probably adjusted quickly.

Nevertheless, the princess undoubtedly heard gossip about Anne and eventually drew her own conclusions about the execution. Her governess probably warned her that it would be prudent to distance herself from the woman who had been convicted of treason against the king; if Elizabeth ever mentioned her mother at all, for the rest of her life, she did so privately.

By custom, princes and princesses lived in separate palaces, a mark of respect

25

Hatfield Royal Palace, the great house in the country where Elizabeth spent much of her childhood. After her death, Robert Cecil, her secretary of state, tore down two wings and used the bricks to build himself a much grander house. The gardens, including the "knot garden" of geometric low hedges, have been designed with contemporary plants in the Elizabethan style.
By kind permission of the Marquess of Salisbury.

for their high position in society. At Hatfield Elizabeth breathed air that was not polluted by the smoke and stench of crowded London, where manure and garbage piled up in the streets and people threw the contents of their chamber pots out the window in the morning. She was also protected by her isolation at Hatfield from infections such as pneumonia, bubonic plague (the Black Death), and "the sweating sickness," the most frequent causes of death. When epidemics flared, no servant was permitted to return to the palace after traveling to London or any other neighborhood where contagion was rampant. Deliveries of food and other goods were left at the gate.

One wing of Hatfield Palace still stands, a rosy-red brick building that houses a vast hall, with a roof two or three stories overhead made of massive chestnut beams. It is a surprisingly rough lodge; in Elizabeth's time the walls no doubt were hung with tapestries, which would have brightened and softened the room and helped hold in the heat. In the two wings that were torn down after Elizabeth's death, each room opened into the next, since hallways were not built in houses then; privacy was unknown. There was probably a "knot garden," with flowers growing between neatly clipped hedges planted in a complicated geometric design.

The forests on the huge estate around the palace were alive with deer. Henry liked to hunt there, as Elizabeth did when she was queen. A few of the oaks that were two hundred years old when she was a child are still alive today, more than four and a half centuries later. Some are so big that three men with their arms outstretched and their hands touching cannot reach around their trunks.

A royal household required many horses and oxen, for animals provided the only land transportation in that time. The crowd of people, sheep, pigs, cattle, chickens, dogs, and other animals that lived with the princess produced huge quantities of garbage and other foul waste. Nobody, not even kings and queens, had running water. Ordinary people used an outdoor toilet called a cesspit. But the princess could hardly be sent outdoors to relieve herself; for her, a chamber pot was placed inside a velvet-covered cabinet hidden behind a bedroom screen or in a small closet. The servant who emptied the chamber pots, called the groom or the lady of the stool, occupied an honored position, as close as anyone could come to a princess's private person.

Foreign visitors to England wrote home with shock about the lack of sanitation, even in the fanciest households. The floors were covered with loose green rushes. People spat on the floor and dropped bones and other scraps for the dogs that waited under the table. Even the cradles of princesses were infested with fleas, and babies' ears and fingers were constantly swollen with itchy red bites. In a climate where apples and buckets of water might freeze in the pantry, where a swan might be butchered in the winter and hung without refrigeration for days or even weeks before it was eaten, houses were heated only by fireplaces. People used screens to protect their faces from the intense heat reflecting from the fire, for they had to sit close to be warm. Babies were tightly wrapped in swaddling clothes, which caused a painful rash.

No rural neighborhood could support a household of one or two hundred people for long, for in a few weeks of residency, the palace bought all available food and ate it. The dung and garbage from the princess's large household piled up as quickly as the food stocks were depleted, and the infestation of fleas and other pests increased. Therefore Elizabeth and the throng of people who lived with her moved constantly from one palace to another so that farmers could cultivate more vegetables and replenish their livestock and servants could shovel out the stables, empty the cesspits, and clean the living quarters.

Though they had their own houses and servants, the king's children spent time at his court as well. As historian Lacey Baldwin Smith points out, a royal court is not a place but a group of people: the king or queen, the officials of the government, and the courtiers and maids of honor who attend the ruler. Wherever the king was living at the moment, there was the court.

Henry may have loved his children, but he was a marvel to be worshipped from a distance, a dictator who held England in his fist. He not only governed the country; he might have been said to own England and his people, having inherited them from his father, who was king before him. And like everybody else in England, Elizabeth was his subject. A visitor who saw father and daughter together reported that she knelt continually. Elizabeth was raised to believe that the king could do no wrong. If Henry put his wife to death, then she must have deserved it.

Small groups of rebels did rise up from time to time. Parliament, with a House of Commons and a House of Lords, was gradually evolving, but government of the people and by the people, historian Smith explains, was unimaginable. Anyone who questioned Henry's right to the English throne merely wanted a different king in his all-powerful place. The idea of an election in the modern sense, with the people deciding who should rule, would have horrified aristocrats and commoners alike. They would have been sure that chaos would result from such a system.

In disinheriting Mary, the king had provided for an orderly transfer of power after his death, and had found a way to keep the throne in his immediate family, despite the lack of a male heir. He had made Anne Boleyn's children the heirs to his kingdom. Unless a son was born, Elizabeth would wear the royal robes and sit on his throne when he died. Although she was a child, she was the child who would be queen, and her servants never forgot that fact for an instant. One day she would hold power over their lives or deaths, as her father held it now. They loved Elizabeth, but there was a distance between them that could not be bridged. They could never give her the warm support of an ordinary loving family.

Now, as suddenly as Elizabeth's mother had died, her father had a new queen, a woman only six years older than Mary. Jane was soon pregnant, and Henry changed the succession again. As he had done to Mary, now he disinherited Elizabeth. Since his marriage to Anne had been annulled when she was tried for treason, Elizabeth was officially the daughter of an unmarried woman, and therefore had no right to the throne. Any children of Jane Seymour's would be Henry's heirs instead. The little strawberry blonde who had been pampered in the sunlight of her father's power and acceptance had now been sent to the shadows. Henry ordered that her servants be "ancient and sad," and the size of her household was reduced to a staff of thirty. Told that she no longer held a royal title, Elizabeth is said to have replied, "How haps it, Governor, that yesterday I was my Lady Princess, and today I am only my Lady Elizabeth?"

The king's officers now oversaw the princess's household. With Elizabeth's

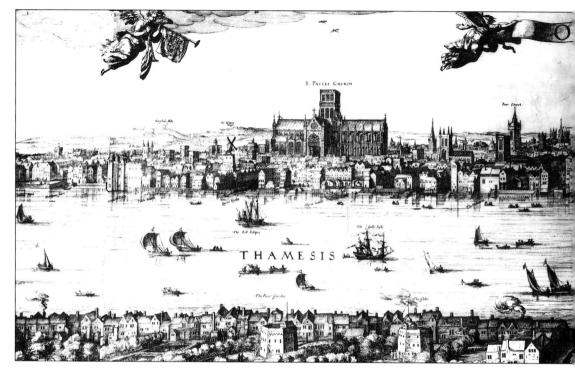

A view of London from the south bank of the Thames. On the far bank is St. Paul's Church,
which later burned. On the near bank are the Globe, where Shakespeare's plays were performed,

mother dead, her governess complained that the council that distributed the king's wealth did not provide enough money to take good care of the little girl. She had been ordered to eat with the adults, even though she was cutting teeth and the food was too rich for her. In such an atmosphere her attendants would not have the authority to teach her proper behavior. The governess wrote a letter to the council saying that the child did not have nightgowns or even decent handkerchiefs.

Soon Jane Seymour's baby was born: a boy at last. At the midnight christening at which her half-brother was named Edward, the four-year-old Elizabeth

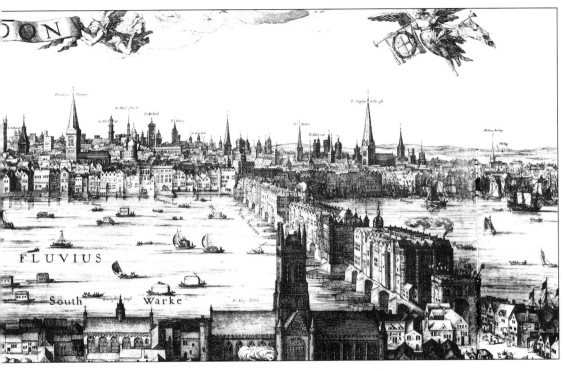

and the Bear Garden. Human heads rotting on poles bristle from the entrance to London Bridge at the right; traffic passed between its elegant shops and houses. MANSELL COLLECTION.

carried his robe in a procession of nobles wrapped in furs and velvet, with gold ornaments that glittered in the candlelight. The robe was so heavy that a nobleman carried her while she carried it. Mary was the prince's godmother; after the christening Elizabeth left the chapel holding her hand. But the joy over the birth of a healthy boy was short-lived. Jane had suffered in labor for three days before the baby was born. Twelve days later, she died of one of the infections that made childbirth a deadly risk then for any woman. Three of England's queens had died in little more than a year.

The young prince sometimes lived with his sisters at Hatfield. Elizabeth was fond of him and made New Year's presents for him. When she was six, she sewed a cambric shirt for him to wear. Soon after, she began writing letters to him in French and Latin.

In 1540, three years after Jane's death, Henry unwillingly married a German woman who could speak no English, Anne of Cleves. That marriage soon ended, and Henry beheaded the official who had arranged it. Nevertheless, Anne of Cleves stayed on in England and played the part of a loving aunt to Henry's children.

King Henry's fifth wife was Katherine Howard, a lively, attractive girl nearly thirty years younger than the king. But that marriage too was doomed. The following winter, under the deep-blue sky and gold stars painted on the ceiling of Henry's private chapel at Hampton Court Palace, a brave courtier told him that Katherine had other lovers. Guards immediately confined her to her rooms, but she escaped and ran screaming through the galleries of the palace, trying to reach the chapel and explain herself to her husband. Henry's men caught her and dragged her back to her apartment.

The king whom some called the cruelest, most dangerous man in Europe ordered her death. Soon she was beheaded, like her cousin Anne Boleyn, among the ravens on the Tower green. As she stood on the scaffold waiting to die, she spoke to the witnesses: "I die a queen, but I would rather die the wife of (her cousin Tom) Culpepper. God have mercy on my soul. Good people, I beg you pray for me."

Elizabeth, now eight and a half years old, was probably protected from these events by her isolation in the country, as she had been from her mother's death. Nevertheless, nothing escaped her notice, and servants do gossip. Everybody remarked on the child's intelligence and seriousness. In six years her father had had four wives; one had died as a result of childbirth, one he had divorced, and two he had beheaded. Elizabeth must have drawn some conclusions about the safety of women and wives and queens.

Occasionally Elizabeth appeared in royal processions or other ceremonies, but usually she led a quiet life at Hatfield or other secluded houses located north of London, away from the hurly-burly, intrigues, and dangers of the court. Her governess, Kate (Katherine Champernowne, who later became Katherine Ashley when she married a relative of Anne Boleyn's), came to serve Elizabeth when the child was four years old. Kate eventually would become first lady of the bedchamber, an honored position in the queen's most private place. They sometimes may have slept in the same bed. A sleeping companion helped a person stay warm in a time when even palaces were cold places, and sixteenth-century people did not like a solitude that felt to them like loneliness.

When Elizabeth was almost ten years old, her father married his sixth and last wife, Katherine Parr. She had been widowed twice and had inherited huge fortunes from both husbands, but she had no children of her own. She took Elizabeth, Mary, and Edward into her care. Once the king banished Elizabeth from court for some mischief that has since been forgotten. Perhaps she was so rash as to say something about her mother or the king's marriages; she always had an acid tongue. Katherine Parr spoke up for her, and months later Henry accepted Lady Elizabeth back into his good graces.

Henry's new wife nursed him as his health failed. Sometimes he put his infected leg across her lap for comfort. But she was his caretaker and his property, not his partner in a marriage of equals. As his other wives had done, she learned the danger of displeasing the king. Sitting with him in her garden, she was so bold as to talk with him about the ideas of the Protestants, those who opposed the power and grandeur of the Roman Catholic Church. Henry told her in a rage, as he had commanded Anne, not to lecture him about religion.

His men moved to arrest her and take her to the Tower. Although Henry stopped them, Katherine knew that the soldiers would not have done so without a signal from him. To ingratiate herself for her own protection, she wrote Henry a groveling letter of apology, saying that she had been misunderstood: She merely wanted him to teach her from his own great knowledge of religion.

Katherine Parr was well educated at a time when learning was not considered important for women, and the common people generally had little regard for books. Her intellectual interests were serious. Because of decisions Katherine made, Elizabeth received the best possible education.

Her half sister, Mary, had been taught by a Spaniard named Vives, who advised teachers never to remove the whipping stick from a boy's back. "The daughter especially shall be handled without cherishing," he wrote. "Cherishing marreth sons, but it utterly destroyeth daughters." This authority on the proper care of children was very influential, and Henry agreed with his ideas. It was thought reasonable that a disobedient child be required to creep across a long gallery on her knees to beg her parents' forgiveness. An ambassador had reported to his government when Henry himself was a boy that the prince feared his father so much, he could only mutter in his presence. The king was said to have beaten the young Henry nearly to death. Rumors may have exaggerated the facts, but the very existence of the rumors alone is striking.

When Elizabeth was six, a messenger brought King Henry's Christmas greetings to her. He reported back that "she gave humble thanks, enquiring again of his majesty's welfare, and that with as great a gravity as [if] she had been forty years old. If she be no worse educated than she now appeareth to me, she will prove of no less honor to womanhood than shall beseem her father's daughter." It would have seemed a compliment to say that a young child was as sober as a forty-year-old woman, for children were appreciated only as creatures who were being molded into adults. From infancy, girls were bound up in corsets and petticoats. Around their necks they wore the same scratchy starched ruffs as their mothers. Boys were similarly rigged out as miniature adults. A painting of Sir Walter Raleigh and his small son (see page 133) depicts them dressed alike, both with swords at their sides.

Children's spirits were also bound. They were punished severely for fighting, spitting, or throwing snowballs. They were also constrained from perfectly benign displays of animation. The renowned scholar Erasmus wrote about children's proper behavior. They must walk as if they had a serious destination, neither rushing nor strolling without a purpose. They must never lean against a wall, jitter or fidget, or wiggle their fingers and toes. They must occupy their hands and arms to keep them at their sides, not allowing them to flap like birds' wings. Children must avoid frowning, wrinkling their noses, yawning, and sniffling. Baby talk was not permitted.

Girls suffered even greater constraints than boys, since people generally assumed that females were inferior creatures who required external controls. No matter "how perfect a woman be either in virtue, beauty, or wealth," according to one contemporary writer, "yet they are to men necessary evils." As little women, girls were thought to be subject to hysteria and controlled by passion and lust. Their morals were scrutinized, and the daughter of the "great whore," Anne Boleyn, must have been observed intensely. People commonly believed that a father had every reason and right to kill an unchaste daughter.

Elizabeth's nursemaids must have been anxious to instill in her a rigid self-control, to drive out any trace of Anne's vivacity in order to protect both Elizabeth and the nursemaids from the king's disapproval. Even ordinary children were admonished not to draw attention to themselves. In the mind of Erasmus, a smile suggested deceit, and laughter looked like madness or wickedness. If laughter was unavoidable, the mouth must be covered, lest the strain twist a child's face. People who sneezed must make the sign of the cross over their lips.

Roger Ascham, who came to teach Elizabeth in her mid adolescence after the death of her first tutor, William Grindal, had different ideas. Some of his other students were Lady Jane Grey, a cousin of the princess, and Robert Dudley, who would become Elizabeth's closest friend. The scholarly Ascham believed in gentleness. "If you pour much drink at once into a goblet," he said, "most of it will overflow. If you pour softly, you may fill it even to the top."

Ascham and his liberal friends at Cambridge University influenced a surge of learning so important that modern people call their historical period, which flowered a century earlier in Italy, the Renaissance, meaning "rebirth." Europe was vibrant with new knowledge of old ideas. Scholars had rediscovered classical literature written in Greek and Latin, the languages of Greece and Rome fifteen centuries and more before Elizabeth was born. The ancients' logic provided the basis for reasoned thought, the foundation for new ways to consider politics and religion. Classicism was at the bottom of the science that would eventually change the world. And the men who taught Elizabeth were at the center of the new thinking.

She rewarded her teachers' efforts, for she was a natural student who always had a book in her hand. Renaissance people admired those who could do all sorts of things so well that they seemed to have been born knowing how. They even had a name for this breadth, *sprezzatura.* Elizabeth therefore took lessons not only in sewing and dancing, manners and horseback riding, but also in mathematics, geography, astronomy, and principles of architecture. She could play a keyboard instrument, the virginals, very well. She loved history above all and studied it for three hours a day, often reading several books about the same period to compare different authors' views. She learned six languages besides English: French, Italian, Spanish, Flemish, Greek, and Latin, and could speak a little Welsh besides. Roger Ascham said that "the brightest star" he ever taught was his "illustrious Lady Elizabeth."

She probably read fluently before she was five or six, since she began then to study Latin. So familiar was she with the classics and other academic subjects that she could converse easily in Latin with her half-brother and -sister, Edward and Mary, who were also brilliant students. But she never learned, as Edward did, the practical knowledge a ruler would need, such as how to supply and command an army, or the management of an economy beginning to explore the New World. She was never taught to lead, for, after Edward's birth, she was not expected to govern. It was thought that Elizabeth would live out her life in obscurity, the mere bastard half-sister of Jane Seymour's prince.

In 1547, when Elizabeth was thirteen, Edward was brought to Enfield, the king's country house, where his sister was staying. A nobleman told them together that King Henry had died. He had been bedridden; his swollen, oozing legs were cauterized with hot irons by a group of physicians who shared responsibility so that no one would be blamed for the death that obviously was coming. Both children burst into tears when they heard the news. The nine-year-old Prince Edward became the new King of England, Edward VI.

And once again Elizabeth's life turned upside down.

King Edward VI, Elizabeth's half-brother, son of Jane Seymour; he inherited the throne at the age of nine, when King Henry VIII died. NATIONAL PORTRAIT GALLERY, LONDON.

4

THE PRINCESS AND THE ADMIRAL

KING HENRY'S WILL HAD ESTABLISHED THE SUCCESSION. First in line for the throne was his only son, Edward, then his elder daughter, Mary. If they should die without heirs, then Elizabeth would be queen.

Next after Henry's own children should have come the heir of his elder sister: her granddaughter Mary, the Queen of Scotland. (The two Marys—Mary Tudor, Elizabeth's half-sister, and the Scottish queen, Elizabeth's distant cousin—are examples of the fact that many girls bore the Virgin Mary's name in Catholic Europe.) Mary, Queen of Scots was nine years younger than Elizabeth and had grown up in the court of France, her mother's homeland. A potential border war was always simmering between England and Scotland, an ally of France. Henry did not want England to fall into the hands of these two Catholic countries, nor did he want a Catholic on the throne of England. For that reason, he left the Scottish Mary out of the succession. Lady Jane Grey, a pious Protestant, the granddaughter of Henry's younger sister, took precedence. This decision was to have great consequences.

Henry had left King Edward and the government in the care of a Protestant council of equals, who were to divide the power among themselves. Jane Seymour's brother, Edward Seymour, dominated, however, and soon became Duke of Somerset and lord protector of the kingdom. He would control the government until the boy king came of age. Edward's other uncle, Thomas Seymour, was appointed lord high admiral.

Katherine Parr had been in love with Tom Seymour when she reluctantly caught King Henry's eye. Not caring to contend with the king over a woman, Seymour had quietly withdrawn, and the widowed Katherine married Henry, her third elderly husband. Thomas Seymour was an opportunist, however. After Henry's death, he sought the council's permission to marry one of the princesses, either Mary or Elizabeth. The council dismissed his schemes to prevent his increasing his power. He seized the next-best advantage. Within four months of the old king's death, Katherine Parr had married Thomas Seymour.

She was overjoyed. "As truly as God is God," she wrote to him, "my mind was fully bent, the other time I was at liberty, to marry you before any man I knew." She had married King Henry against her own wishes. Now it seemed that her submission and patience had been rewarded. "God," she said, "is a marvelous man."

Thomas Seymour's jealousy of his elder brother, with whom the admiral wanted to share the protectorate, caused constant dissension. As soon as he married, Thomas gained control of Elizabeth, since she was being educated in Katherine's household. Then he made a substantial loan without interest to the father of ten-year-old Jane Grey and moved her in with Katherine and himself as well. Girls were even less free then than they are today to choose where they would live. Mary lived in a separate household. But now King Henry's widow and two of the heirs to his throne—Elizabeth and Jane—were overseen by Thomas Seymour. He also tried to gain the loyalty, if not the custody, of King Edward.

The admiral was a man as handsome and attractive as he was ambitious. His bold exuberance won over other people. At the age of fourteen, Elizabeth was not immune to his charm. He began to tease her by coming to her chamber, "bare legged in his slippers" and wearing only a nightgown, in the morning before she was up. He shook the curtains around her bed and feigned as if to climb in with her. She blushed and pulled the coverlet up to her chin.

If she was up and dressed, as she often arranged to be for her own protection, "he would bid her good morrow, and ask how she did, and strike her upon the back or on the buttocks familiarly." When he "strove to have kissed her in her bed," Kate Ashley "bade him go away for shame."

Mrs. Ashley told Katherine that people were gossiping about this unseemly horseplay with the princess, but the queen did not stop it. Instead, she joined in. Twice she came with Thomas "and there they tickled my lady Elizabeth in the bed, the queen and my lord Admiral." Another time Thomas found Elizabeth in the garden, "wrestled with her and cut her gown in an hundred pieces" with his sword. When Mrs. Ashley scolded her, the girl said that she had been unable to escape, for "the Queen held her, while the Lord Admiral cut" her black dress.

Thomas Seymour and Elizabeth's stepmother may have been trying to promote playfulness in a girl who had acted like a woman of forty when she was six years old. If so, they were certainly indiscreet. Elizabeth heard the lock click at the door one morning and knew that the admiral, who had keys to all the doors in the house, was coming. To evade him, she "ran out of her bed to her maidens, and then went behind the curtain of the bed, the maidens being there; and my lord tarried to have her come out." Afterward Mrs. Ashley stopped the admiral in the gallery and told him that people were gossiping about him and saying evil things about Elizabeth's morals.

That winter Elizabeth and Mary went to court and spent Christmas with their brother. An Italian traveler had noticed the extreme deference shown the king when he was but ten years old. "I have seen, for example, the Princess Elizabeth drop on one knee five times before her brother, before she took her place" at dinner on a cushioned bench down the table from Edward's chair and canopy.

Even when they conversed in private, Elizabeth and Mary were on their knees, unless the boy bade them sit with him. Having been raised in the court of the all-powerful Henry, however, the king's sisters were accustomed to paying deference. Doing otherwise would have seemed unnatural.

Early in the summer Katherine, pregnant with Thomas Seymour's child, suddenly sent away Elizabeth and her household, which had grown now to more than one hundred people. According to the story told later, the queen had come into a room and found her husband with her adolescent stepdaughter in his arms. Katherine must have been shocked; she had not intended the games to become a romance.

This indiscretion was not petty. Since children born to any of the Tudors would affect the succession, the balance of power, and the future of everyone in the kingdom, the sexual behavior of princesses was a political matter in which Parliament took a deep interest. Moreover, a princess who was not a virgin had lost her value as a product on the royal marriage market. If the admiral made advances to Elizabeth, he had violated his trust as the caretaker of a child young enough to have been his daughter—though old enough, at fourteen, to be another man's wife.

Everyone "knew," as people had once "known" that the world was flat, that females were naturally inclined to laziness and loose morals. And Elizabeth's character was further tainted in the public mind by her mother's reputation, no matter how virtuous she herself might be. People watched her closely, always expecting the worst. A further scandal, in addition to her scandalous birth, would destroy her.

Perhaps the reckless Thomas Seymour enjoyed the very danger of his flirtation with an heir to the throne. Whether he began these antics as a joke or as something more serious, however, he went too far. Nor did he learn prudence from experience. The admiral had courted King Edward's affection, writing to him secretly and sending him pocket money in letters that mentioned the protector's stinginess. Now Thomas Seymour began to talk about raising popular support in a way that sounded like rebellion against his brother.

Queen Katherine died within a week of her baby girl's birth, probably of the same kind of massive infection that had killed Jane Seymour, King Edward's mother. Now, at fifteen, Elizabeth was alone in a dangerous world, with no powerful sponsors to protect her, for the king himself was in the power of a manipulative man who cared nothing for Edward's sisters. And soon the romantic Kate Ashley was urging her to accept the admiral's courtship.

Thomas Seymour met in London with the treasurer of Elizabeth's house, Thomas Parry, and asked searching questions about her financial affairs. How much land did she own? Where was it located? How much income did it bring? Such questions mattered to a future husband, for whatever belonged to the girl would become his when they married. Elizabeth was no fool, however; she ignored her servants' plans.

Without the defense of Queen Katherine's privileged position and the goodwill of her friends, Thomas Seymour's impetuous character brought him down. Four months after Katherine's death, he was sent to the Tower for treason. He had tried to seize King Edward at night, but the boy's little dog barked and roused the guards. Now Seymour was accused of political crimes. Kate Ashley and Thomas Parry were imprisoned for interrogation.

At the age of fifteen, Elizabeth was already a mature observer of politics and intrigue. She could read the hidden meaning of words and actions and keep a cool head in a crisis that might have meant her imprisonment as an accomplice to Seymour's treason. Although the stories of her romps with the admiral must have mortified her, she refused to blame her servants, scorned their reports as mere backstairs gossip, and denied that Seymour had ever proposed marriage to her. Indeed he had not; knowing danger when she saw it, she had spurned all conversation on the matter with Mrs. Ashley and Thomas Parry and had avoided anything that looked like secret negotiations.

Elizabeth turned around the government's suspicions of her with masterful letters to the protector, declaring that she had nothing to hide and demanding that he silence the lewd tongues that were wagging everywhere, gossiping that she was pregnant with the admiral's child and had been imprisoned in the Tower. She wanted to go to court and show herself as she was, a virtuous maid. Already Elizabeth had grasped the value of her people's good opinion. Already she understood how vital were appearances. For the rest of her life, she would woo the English, knowing that their love and respect would be her shield against danger. Eventually she would endear herself to them with the image of Good Queen Bess and counter gossip with the myth of the Virgin Queen.

Elizabeth thereafter played the role of virtuous maiden, presenting herself in simple clothing with little adornment in a time when courtiers spent fortunes for the pearls on their shoes. When other ladies of the court dressed in vivid colors, she wore simple black and white. In an age of opulence, simplicity set her apart and even called attention to itself. Her style was partly a matter of economy, for she did not have more money than she needed to keep her huge household going, though she was anything but poor. A surviving household account puts her yearly income at 4,800 pounds. (If an English pound at the time was, as one historian estimates, worth 500 modern pounds, then she received the equivalent of 2,400,000 modern English pounds per year.)

Her own lands supplied the needs of her kitchen—such necessities as wheat, barley, and eggs. A wide variety of meat came from the farms, including veal and beef, pork and mutton, goose, duck, and chicken, as well as wild game hunted in her own forests. Visitors also brought her delicacies as gifts; some scholars gave her apples, and a woman brought a basket of spring peas. In one season, according to surviving records, Elizabeth bought new brooms, a Bible, lute strings, and a small walnut table. She kept musicians in her household, but she did not spend money on jewels and gowns.

Whether or not the effect was calculated, her relative simplicity appealed to the Protestants. Mary gave Jane Grey an exquisite gown of tinsel cloth of gold and velvet, decorated with gold lace made of the precious metal itself. "What shall I do with it?" Jane asked. Wear it, her ladies said. But Jane associated Mary's and Elizabeth's different styles of dress with the differences in their religion— Mary's ornate clothing reflected her attachment to the old ceremonial ways, while Elizabeth wore plainness as a badge of her Protestantism. "Nay," Jane said, she couldn't wear the gown; "that were a shame to follow my Lady Mary against God's word, and leave my Lady Elizabeth, which followeth God's word."

Elizabeth had a ferocious temper, but she reined in her sharp tongue and her haughty manner, knowing that they were dangerous to her, and behaved in a modest way that matched her modest dress. When a foreign ambassador paid her a visit at Hatfield Royal Palace, she informed the government immediately, lest she do anything that seemed important without its being known to everyone. Her brother called her his "sweet sister Temperance."

Anne Boleyn's daughter saved herself with prudence and courage, having learned lessons from Anne's career and her own experience. But Thomas Seymour was rash to the end, refusing his brother's invitation to confer privately, a meeting that might have saved the admiral. Soon he was beheaded. When Elizabeth heard of his death, she is said to have observed, "This day died a man of much wit but little judgment."

In Tudor England a beaten politician did not withdraw quietly to the country to lick his wounds. There was no such thing as a "loyal opposition" in government. Powerful leaders who lost their power were considered too dangerous to live. Within a year and a half the protector himself, Edward Seymour, the Duke of Somerset, had been beheaded for treason, brought down by the Earl of Warwick, John Dudley, the father of Elizabeth's friend Robert. John Dudley soon became lord protector and Duke of Northumberland.

During the tumult accompanying these executions, King Edward remained aloof, coolly detached while his own uncles were beheaded. He even brought evidence against Thomas Seymour. The king's mother had died at his birth and his father when Edward was nine. Thereafter his life was even less his own than it had been when he was merely being spoiled as the heir to the throne. At least when he was younger, he had been permitted the companionship of sisters, who by all accounts doted on him. But as king he was manipulated by politicians. There were stories of Edward's coldness and cruelty and his self-righteous piety. He was said to have plucked the feathers from a live falcon that perched in his bedroom. Then he tore it into pieces, telling his tutors that "he likened himself to the falcon, whom everybody plucked, but that he would pluck them too hereafter, and tear them in four parts." Like Elizabeth, Edward had not survived the pain of his own childhood without damage.

With avid Protestants in power, the government replaced the elaborate rituals of the Catholics with simpler religious services. The bread and wine of the sacrament were now seen as a commemoration of Jesus' death rather than his literal body and blood. Resenting these radical changes in their spiritual lives, changes that had been forced upon them, the common people rioted in the streets of London. And Mary was devastated by the further destruction of the faith she held dear. She began to plot escape from England in order to find sanctuary with the Hapsburg emperor, her cousin Charles V. Ships were even sent for her, but she lost her nerve. Failing to escape, she illegally kept a priest in her house and held Mass in secret, sorrowing for her countrymen.

In 1552, when Elizabeth was eighteen, King Edward fell ill with smallpox and measles. By autumn, he was pale and thin, suffering from "galloping consumption," a virulent tuberculosis that progressed rapidly toward death. Elizabeth worried about her brother, but Northumberland kept her away from court, to prevent her interference with his plans for the succession.

In an attempt to consolidate his power in April 1553, the duke arranged the marriage of his son Guilford Dudley to the fifteen-year-old Jane Grey; he hoped for the birth of a male heir while the sick king still lived. Although Jane detested the Dudleys, her abusive parents forced her to marry a man she despised. Some people believe that the duke also hired a quack to dose the king with arsenic. That treatment would poison the boy and prolong his agony, but, Northumberland hoped, would also keep him alive on the throne while the duke maneuvered Guilford and Jane to inherit the crown.

Lady Jane Grey, Elizabeth's distant cousin, who, at the age of fifteen, was involved against her will in schemes to usurp the crown. Nine days into Jane's reign, Elizabeth's half-sister raised an army and took her place as Queen Mary I. The following year, she had Jane beheaded. NATIONAL PORTRAIT GALLERY, LONDON.

Knowing that Mary would restore Roman Catholicism if she were queen, the Protestant King Edward declared that Mary and Elizabeth were only his illegitimate half-sisters, and that the foreign princes they would likely marry would subvert England to another country's advantage. Nobody knows whether he acted willingly, but he was certainly manipulated by John Dudley, Duke of Northumberland, who had isolated the king from his sisters. As a minor, Edward had no legal standing to change the order of succession his father had decided and Parliament had sanctioned; indeed such an act would have been treasonous. Nevertheless, Edward excluded Mary and Elizabeth from the succession. The document he wrote named Jane Grey and her sisters his heirs.

5
BLOODY MARY

ᴍEDICAL KNOWLEDGE WAS SKETCHY and treatment primitive in Tudor England. Physicians "bled" people for all sorts of maladies, using leeches or slitting veins and collecting the blood in basins. One "cure" was to swallow a live spider in molasses. As treatment for another condition, a pullet, a live young chicken, was tied to the patient's body until the bird died.

Royalty as well as common people suffered from the ignorance of physicians. On July 6, 1553, King Edward VI, the last of the Tudor kings, died a terrible death at Greenwich Royal Palace. Having willed his throne to Lady Jane Grey, he and his officials had undone all of King Henry's efforts to assure a peaceful transfer of power through a clearly lawful succession.

The Duke of Northumberland suppressed the news of King Edward's death and summoned Mary and Elizabeth, hoping to lure them into a trap and imprison them. A secret friend at court sent riders to warn them that the duke had carried out a palace revolution.

Mary barely avoided capture by Robert Dudley, Elizabeth's friend and

Northumberland's son, who had pursued her with a troop of horsemen. Sheltered in a castle, she called her people to arms. Now each person's future depended upon a crucial judgment. Who was likely to triumph in this contest, the courtiers must have asked themselves, the powerful Northumberland and his puppet, Queen Jane, or the small, retiring Mary, the rightful heir to the throne? Those who stood now with the future winner would prosper, while those who miscalculated would be ruined.

Elizabeth knew that she was cornered. If she supported Mary as queen and Northumberland won, Elizabeth's own life would be worth nothing. If she supported Jane and Mary won, Mary would destroy her. Northumberland sent courtiers to Elizabeth at Hatfield. Offered a bribe to renounce her right to the crown and embrace Queen Jane, Elizabeth remained neutral, clinging to a strict interpretation of the succession. She herself had no claim to give up while Mary lived, she told the messengers; they must deal with Mary.

Military power was on Northumberland's side, but he had not reckoned with Mary's bravery, nor had he accurately gauged the people's hostility to him and their affection for her. He had earned the everlasting hatred of Catholics with his harsh religious policies. As soon as he rode out of London with his army, his allies abandoned him, and his shaky government collapsed. Northumberland was arrested and imprisoned in the Tower with the three sons, including Robert, who had pursued Mary. They carved an emblem with a bear and other family symbols in the stone wall of their cell, which remains there today. The duke was beheaded, but Mary spared his three sons and Jane Grey, who had occupied the throne for nine short days. She too went to a prison cell in the Tower of London.

Edward's council, which had bent to Northumberland's pressure, now hastily proclaimed Mary queen, England's first crowned queen. On July 31, 1553, she made her way to London, where Elizabeth rode to meet her, accompanied by two thousand horsemen, and joined the triumphant march to the Tower. Mary was thirty-seven years old, Elizabeth not yet twenty.

Elizabeth had made all the right moves. She had refused to take advantage of Mary's trouble. Then she made a great public show of her respect and loyalty as Mary's subject the moment the new queen arrived in London. At first the sisters were affectionate. Mary held Elizabeth's hand at court affairs and accorded her the place of honor at state occasions.

Everyone said that Mary was an exceptionally softhearted woman, but unyielding in matters of religion. She was certain that God had appointed her queen for a purpose. It was her duty to lead England and all her subjects back to the true Church. Under Henry's threat she had denied her faith, but now God had given her a second chance.

Mary had led a sheltered life among Roman Catholic believers. It was easy for her to suppose that the religious changes made during Edward's reign were superficial. But Mary was wrong. Noblemen who had received the monasteries' lands and other wealth were unwilling to give them back. The government had capitalized on a hatred of foreigners by making the seizure of the Church's power and wealth seem like a patriotic act. People had taken pride in King Henry's defiance of the papacy. When Londoners welcomed Mary, they rejoiced at their own freedom from Northumberland's dictatorship. While they were relieved to see the traditional line of succession honored, however, they would never again tolerate control by a foreign pope.

Mary and the Catholics regretted the difficulty of restoring Catholicism, while Protestants were dissatisfied that reform was not going forward. Extremists attacked priests. Mobs destroyed altars and crosses and pounded the stone carvings in churches with chains and hammers until the sculpted figures were unrecognizable. (These scars can still be seen in English churches.) Within a month of Mary's accession, Londoners organized violent demonstrations in the streets.

Mary announced that she had no wish to "compel or restrain other men's consciences," but she trusted that God would lead them to the truth—*her* truth. Although Mass was still officially illegal, priests celebrated it openly at court six or seven times a day. Elizabeth stayed away from these services, trying to avoid entanglement on either side.

She was the hope of the Protestants, who wanted her support of their cause, and although she always loved ritual and ceremony, she was sympathetic to them. She had never known the old religion, after all; her mother and Katherine Parr had been Protestants, and Protestant tutors had educated her. A Catholic queen held power now, however, and Protestantism was dangerous, especially to Elizabeth, for it made her the focus of rebellion. She could not give open support to those who opposed Queen Mary.

Neither could Elizabeth embrace Catholicism. If she had done so, she would have admitted that the annulment of Henry's marriage to Catherine of Aragon was illegal and consequently that she herself was a bastard with no right to the throne. All her life, Elizabeth was careful not to call attention to the circumstances of her birth. She walked a narrow path; a misstep on either side would bring down ruin on her, if not death.

By August antagonism between the half-sisters was evident. Knowing that Elizabeth was not attending Mass, Mary became cold to her. Elizabeth requested a meeting with Mary at which she wept on her knees and claimed ignorance because of her Protestant upbringing. She asked for books and instruction. Mary ordered her to attend Mass. She went, but she complained of a stomachache as she walked all the way through the palace to the chapel.

Mary relied for counsel on the Spanish ambassador, Simon Renard. He had unsuccessfully urged Jane Grey's execution. He was even more afraid of Elizabeth, thinking her a sly heretic who, drawing discontent without trying, was too dangerous to remain free. She would use religion as a political weapon, he warned Mary. Henry had executed everyone who might have threatened his power, and Mary ought to do the same for her own safety.

"The Princess Elizabeth is greatly to be feared," Renard wrote his government. "She has a spirit full of enchantment." Her manner was regal; she towered over the tiny Mary and looked more like a queen than the queen herself. "An air of dignified majesty pervades all her actions," wrote another diplomat. "No one can fail to suppose she is a queen."

Mary admitted that she could not forget her hatred for "the concubine's daughter," but her despised half-sister was nonetheless her heir. In the place of honor at Mary's coronation, Elizabeth complained about the weight of her gold coronet. Never mind, the French ambassador said; soon this crown would bring a better one.

The Frenchman's joke was a reminder that France posed another danger to Mary Tudor. Her cousin Mary, Queen of Scots, who was now nearly twelve years old, had an excellent legal claim to the crown. Despite Henry's exclusion of her family from his will, nothing could change the fact that she was the granddaughter of his elder sister and therefore, according to the rules of succession, next in line for the throne after Henry's own legitimate children. The Scottish Mary, a Catholic like Mary Tudor, was to marry the eldest son of the French king. What a comfort to France it would be if the future king's wife were the queen of both Scotland and England; the alliance would protect France from its neighbor, Spain. France therefore had an interest in placing its own candidate on the throne of England, displacing a daughter Henry VIII had once declared a bastard.

One of Mary Tudor's first acts was to repeal the annulment of her parents' marriage, legally asserting her own legitimacy and Elizabeth's bastardy. And the first Parliament of the new reign reversed all of King Edward's Protestant laws. The Tudors had a liking for legal decisions that overthrew their predecessors' hard-fought positions. Throughout her first twenty-five years, Elizabeth was alternately legitimized and bastardized, recognized as heir to the throne and disinherited, favored and kicked out so many times that one can hardly keep track of her standing. The constant jerks in her status must have made her reel, uncertain from moment to moment whether she was doomed or blessed.

Try as Mary would to treat her half-sister civilly, her loathing still came out. Elizabeth liked to wear a tiny gold book containing the Protestant prayer King Edward had made on his deathbed. Of course, Mary hated all Protestant prayers, no matter who prayed them. She sent Elizabeth a gift. It was a gold ornament to be worn at Elizabeth's waist, containing miniature portraits of Henry and Catherine of Aragon, Queen Mary's mother, whom Anne Boleyn had displaced. Elizabeth trembled when Mary talked to her; she may have been compelled by fear to wear this cruel reminder of her parentage.

The queen told her courtiers in a rage that Henry was not Elizabeth's father. The scandal would disgrace the kingdom if such a hypocritical heretic bastard were ever crowned. Renard urged Mary to imprison Elizabeth in the Tower. When he listed Mary's four enemies at the beginning of her reign, one was France, another Elizabeth.

Mary was indeed in danger, but her courage and spirit were famous. Despite assassination threats, she attended public events openly, as if she faced no risk. Once, when she and Elizabeth were walking through the palace to vespers, someone nearby shouted, "Treason!" Mary went on without blinking. Elizabeth was so frightened that she paled and trembled and "could not compose her countenance." She asked her companion to rub her stomach to calm her before she joined the queen in the chapel.

Soon Mary had given precedence at court to their cousin Margaret, the Catholic Countess of Lennox and daughter of Henry VIII's sister Margaret. The countess's son, Henry Stuart, Lord Darnley, had a place in the line of succession.

Mary gave the countess a seat nearby at her table and an equally prominent position at other ceremonies. Elizabeth's loss of prestige was more than a public insult. It was a cue to everybody, courtiers and commoners alike, that she no longer had the queen's favor. Appearances were power. Loss of the ruler's favor meant actual loss of power, which might be an omen of Elizabeth's imprisonment or death.

Rather than be publicly snubbed, Elizabeth asked permission to live quietly in the country, promising to keep priests in her household and to dismiss any servants she suspected of opposing Mary's reign. She would "do all in her power to please the Queen." Renard wrote to Emperor Charles V that "care was being taken to have [Elizabeth's] every action observed."

Mary Tudor had no intention of allowing Elizabeth to succeed her on the throne. It was her duty to God and country to give birth to children who would follow her in the Catholic faith. To that purpose she decided to marry Philip of Spain, the son of her cousin the emperor. Everyone had assumed that she would marry, of course; it was out of the question that a woman might rule England alone. Mary must have a husband to take care of "those duties which were not the province of ladies."

Her councilors were unhappy with her choice of husband, however. Fearful of being drawn into foreign wars, they begged her to marry an Englishman. Both houses of Parliament sent delegations expressing their horror at the prospect of seeing a Spaniard at the queen's side. Mary told them all that her choice was nobody's business but her own. She wanted an equal and her mother's kinsman as her husband, a man of royal blood, not a subject. Ignoring his reputation for promiscuity and a "sinister and taciturn disposition," she would marry Philip or nobody.

In January 1554 the marriage treaty was signed. The bridegroom sent letters to Mary's council signed "Philippus Rex"—King Philip—presuming to name himself their king before he had even married their queen. The tactful Renard

Philip, son of Catherine of Aragon's nephew and eventually king of Spain. He married Queen Mary I, his distant cousin, a woman he had seen only in a flattering portrait. NATIONAL POR-TRAIT GALLERY, LONDON.

destroyed the letters and delivered their contents personally. It was well that Philip's presumption was not known, for the people began to panic as it was. A dead dog with its hair cut like a priest's had been thrown into Mary's chamber. Cries were heard in the street: "We will have no foreigner for our King!" Rebellion was rumbling through England.

While demonstrations against the announced marriage plans increased, several plotters, including Thomas Wyatt, Edward Courtenay, and Jane Grey's father, planned an uprising. Wyatt was a Catholic knight who had supported Mary's claim to the throne, but he hated Spaniards and was determined to keep them out of England. Courtenay, a Catholic descended from Elizabeth's great-grand-father, had grown up as a prisoner in the Tower after Henry VIII executed his father. The conspirators would march on London, supported by a popular uprising. Perhaps they planned that Elizabeth would marry Courtenay and seize Mary's throne.

Although Elizabeth later swore in writing and on her knees and before taking the sacrament that she had received no word of this plot, she was not completely ignorant of Wyatt's intentions, for she protected Ashridge, one of her country mansions, with armed men. Whether she joined it or not, any such conspiracy risked Elizabeth's life.

The rebels may have hoped that Mary would flee London and leave an unreliable army to face the siege. Though she was a queen, she was a woman, nonetheless, thought incapable of courage in battle. Many of Mary's soldiers had already gone over to the enemy, shouting, "We are all Englishmen!" But Mary was always at her best at the worst of times, when underlying trouble came out into the open. Instead of fleeing, she stayed to rally her men and fight. She rode to the Guildhall at the center of London. Her deep voice rang in a fiery speech that roused the city.

The scheme discovered, Courtenay confessed, forcing Wyatt to act on January 25, 1554, before he was ready. Mary's army crushed him before he reached the city. Now she realized that some survivors of Northumberland's conspiracy, whom she had spared in mercy, were too dangerous to live. Jane Grey's mere presence in the world posed a threat to Mary's life. Like Elizabeth's, her very existence focused the discontent of the people, enabling them to imagine a different queen. "Every day someone is condemned to death," an ambassador reported to his government. "This one has been executed; yet another has been taken prisoner." Jane and her father were beheaded, and the government built gallows throughout the city to hang Wyatt's rebels. The soldiers who had gone over to him were hanged in the streets outside their houses.

If Mary would kill the sixteen-year-old Jane, whom she had known fondly since infancy, what would she do to Elizabeth, whose life constantly reminded Mary of her father's betrayal? It was Elizabeth who would have profited most from Wyatt's triumph. Having broken the rebellion, Mary sent physicians and courtiers in February to bring her sister to court, where she could be guarded and, if she proved to have been involved in the conspiracy, punished.

Elizabeth had suffered intermittently from migraine headaches. Now she had been bedridden for some time with a serious kidney disease. Although Mary's physicians reported that she could be moved, she was so weak that she nearly fainted as she entered the queen's litter. The company traveled slowly, going only thirty miles in ten days, but Elizabeth would have welcomed a crawl. Jane had been beheaded the day the journey began; Elizabeth must have thought that she was going to her own execution too.

On the gates of London hung the quartered bodies of Wyatt's rebels, and the entry bristled with heads on pikes, a grisly lesson to Mary's potential enemies. As Elizabeth passed through this horror, she ordered that the curtains of her litter be drawn back. Dressed in white, her face and arms extremely swollen and pale, she was visibly ill. She may have wished to see the people of London, to assess her position with them. Surely she also wished that they should see her.

Elizabeth was a master propagandist who knew from an early age how to summon the people's support. As she knew herself to be in danger, her people must witness that Mary had forced her to travel under escort during an illness. Ambassador Renard wrote that Elizabeth's "look [was] proud, lofty and superbly disdainful."

Her arrival at Whitehall Palace was quiet. Mary did not wish to see her and had assigned her to isolated rooms where she could neither talk with others nor see them. Soon Wyatt was tried, convicted, and hanged; his body was quartered and displayed as a warning to other rebellious citizens, but people who considered him a martyr for England stole his head. Exiled, Courtenay later would die of an infection. Two days after Wyatt's execution, Mary's noblemen came to take Elizabeth to prison.

6
SUBJECT TO HER SISTER

THE COURTIERS who came to imprison Elizabeth in the Tower of London had known her all her life. They remembered her father dancing the beribboned baby through the palace galleries. They had held the child's hand under the brightly colored banners at tournaments. When she was in her teens, they had ridden horses at her side and shot stags with crossbows.

But now Elizabeth was twenty years old and suspected of conspiring against Queen Mary's life. Having commanded her to court, Mary first refused to see her and then ordered her locked in the Tower of London. The councilors dismissed all but six of Elizabeth's own servants and six others loyal to the queen.

On the morning of March 17, with the palace surrounded by soldiers to prevent the escape of the heir to the throne, Mary's men came to escort Elizabeth to the Tower. One was her uncle, Henry, Earl of Sussex; his mother had been a Howard. Seeing her terror, these men were careful and polite, but firm. Disobedience to the queen would endanger themselves.

Elizabeth feared that she was going to her death. She asked again to speak with her sister, hoping to move Mary to mercy, but the courtiers refused. Elizabeth begged to write a letter. The courtiers doubtfully relented. With a goose-quill pen and ink, taking great care with the elegant script she had practiced since early childhood, Elizabeth wrote that she was her sister's loyal subject, innocent of treachery, who would always serve the queen:

> I never practiced, counseled, nor consented to anything that might be prejudicial to your person any way or dangerous to the state by any means. I pray God I may die the shamefullest death that ever any died before if I may mean [intend] any such thing. . . . Let conscience move your Highness to take some better way with me than to make me be condemned in all men's sight afore my desert [the reward or punishment I deserve be] known.

In her anxiety Elizabeth omitted words and made mistakes unusual in her writing. If Wyatt had sent her a letter, she said, she had never received it, nor had she ever written to the French king, as had been charged. She begged Mary to speak with her about any accusations before believing them.

Taking her time, writing slowly, perhaps Elizabeth hoped that, if she delayed her departure long enough, the barge waiting to carry her to the Tower would be unable to depart. People who might see King Henry's younger daughter brought to the Tower through the streets of London would be roused to sympathy for her. Therefore the courtiers planned to take her to prison by water, along the same route her mother had followed to her death.

The Thames was London's main highway, busy with boats carrying freight and passengers up and down on the tide. Palaces and noblemen's mansions, fish markets, theaters, and wool depots were all located on the riverbank. But as the tide in the river rose and fell, the water flowing between the piers of London Bridge became so dangerously rapid that boat traffic was delayed.

Elizabeth's letter covered one page and part of a second. Between the end of the message and her signature, she drew diagonal lines to prevent others from forging additional words. At the bottom, she wrote, "I humbly crave but one word of answer from yourself. Your Highness's most faithful subject that hath been from the beginning and will be [to] my end, Elizabeth."

The courtiers carried the letter to the queen while they waited for the tide to turn, but Mary furiously refused to read the message. From her own experience during Edward's reign, she knew that the heir to the throne attracted treason as honey draws flies. Mary did not trust Elizabeth's well-known charm and cleverness.

The following morning, a cold and drizzly Palm Sunday, the courtiers escorted Princess Elizabeth to the water stairs where the royal barge waited. Elizabeth saw prisoners chained and exposed to the cold and rain on the riverbank. The barge passed under the shops and elegant houses of London Bridge, where the heads of traitors rotted on poles. At the Tower, the river lapped the highest stone step at the water's edge. As Elizabeth splashed out of the barge at the landing that later came to be known as the Traitors' Gate, one of the courtiers offered his cloak to protect the princess from the rain. Angry, she pushed his hand away and, sitting down on a stone, refused to move.

"Come," said a kind lieutenant. "This is an unhealthy place to sit."

"Better sit here than in a worse place," Elizabeth answered, "for God knows where you will bring me."

One of her own men began to weep. She scolded him. Since she was innocent, she said, God would protect her. Nevertheless, whatever God thought, she was at the prison gate. When one of the men appealed to her dignity as a princess, she crossed the green and climbed the stone steps to the second floor of the sixty-foot Bell Tower. A courtier moved to lock the door behind her;

The Traitors' Gate, where Anne Boleyn and Elizabeth entered the Tower of London, has been blocked with stone, as this view from the Thames shows. The government plans to reopen the Gate and the moat that surrounds the Tower. MALCOLM CROWTHERS.

another reminded him that Elizabeth was heir to the throne. *They* might be in *her* power someday. The man left the door unlocked.

For two months, expecting the executioner to cut off her head at any moment, Elizabeth remained a captive in the uppermost room of the Bell Tower, built centuries earlier of creamy stone. Her cell was just above the one where King Henry's friend Thomas More had waited to die. Edward Courtenay had also been imprisoned there. Smoky torches, candles, and three high arched windows lit the circular room. Elizabeth's ladies brought bright rugs worked in geometric designs, and tapestries for the walls. Her own trusted servants cooked her food to be sure that nobody poisoned their mistress. The toilet was a hole in the castle wall through which waste fell into the moat below. A fireplace provided heat.

But nothing could warm Elizabeth's heart against the chilling knowledge of what once had happened among the ravens on the brilliant green lawn below. There, in the midst of May birdsong and roses, her mother, Anne Boleyn, had been beheaded at the order of Elizabeth's own father, King Henry. Beside that lawn stood the church where Anne had been buried in a crude wooden box meant for arrows.

Living in such ghost-haunted conditions, Elizabeth did not recover; her illness worsened. The guards refused to give her paper and pen, for fear that she might try to write to Mary again or gather the support of friends. But she was allowed at last to exercise on the battlements of the castle. Every day she walked with two men before her and two men behind, past the windows of the oak-paneled chamber where her mother, some think, had awaited death. The name *Anne* is visible today, carved in the stone above the fireplace.

At the other end of the walkway was Beauchamps Tower. Robert Dudley was still imprisoned there with his brothers. Elizabeth may have encountered her friend in the Tower, but it is not likely. Still, she probably knew where he was. Certainly she saw, across the moat, Londoners who could glimpse her as she passed the notches in the castle wall. She must have hoped that Mary would fear those people if she killed the heir to the throne; at the same time, too much sympathy for Elizabeth would make Mary fear her lifelong rival all the more.

As spring came on and Elizabeth gradually recovered, the guards allowed her to sit in a small enclosed garden, where she befriended a four-year-old boy, son of a Tower official. Fearful that the naive child might carry messages to and from the princess, the guards forbade him to speak to her again. At night she lay awake, smelling the cages and listening to the screeches and bellows of the animals in the royal zoo down the hill. A stench hung over the Tower of London, even in the coolness of March and April, for the moat surrounding it was below the water level of the river. The floating garbage and waste flowed into the moat and remained there when the ocean tides cleansed the river mouth.

Under torture on the rack, Wyatt and his men had proclaimed that Elizabeth was not a party to the rebellion. Katherine Ashley, the governess who had served Elizabeth since she was four years old, resisted questioning by the queen's men and upheld her mistress's innocence. In his last words before he died, Wyatt insisted upon Elizabeth's innocence. Their steadfast defense of her would help her cause.

Still, when she heard soldiers marching on the green below her Tower window, Elizabeth asked whether Jane Grey's scaffold still stood, wondering whether it would be used for her own execution. The constable of the Tower changed during her stay; she asked whether the new man was the sort who would follow an order to murder a prisoner secretly.

On May 19, the eighteenth anniversary of her mother's beheading, Elizabeth was ordered to ready herself for travel. She thought that she would be taken to a remote place for secret execution. "This night I think to die," she told a servant. Her escort assured her that she need fear nothing from him. The investigation having proven no involvement by Elizabeth in Wyatt's uprising, Queen Mary had released her to house arrest at the gatehouse of a decrepit manor at Woodstock. People heard that she was coming. They gathered at the side of the road to hand her May flowers and cakes and meat pies and to call out their good wishes. They filled her litter with gifts until there was hardly room for the princess, and she had to ask them to stop.

Space at Woodstock was so limited that Elizabeth's servants lodged in the town. Soon her treasurer, Mr. Parry, had set up a sort of headquarters at the inn, where information passed in and out. The princess had been accustomed to a robust outdoor life before her imprisonment. People near her estates knew her, for she loved to ride, even in cold and rainy weather. Now this active young woman was restricted to four rooms in a cramped house without entertainment, with only occasional walks in the gardens for exercise.

Mary had replaced Elizabeth's women, even her favorite companion, with servants loyal to the queen. The roof leaked, and the house was damp and cold, with insufficient wood in the region to keep the fires going. Sometimes, Elizabeth said, her hands were so cold and she shivered so much that she could not seal a letter. The cold made her illness recur, but when she asked to see the royal physicians, something prevented their coming. She could make do, they said, with the treatment of local doctors. Elizabeth declined. She would rather die than be examined by ordinary men, she said.

The ill-tempered young woman bedeviled her jailer with alternating silences and tirades. She smuggled in forbidden books, though everything that came into the house was searched except her underwear. She demanded an English Bible (a Protestant book), and complained about the spying women Mary had sent to serve her. Despite her poor health, she argued that she had received Mary's permission to ride and walk in the park. But her keeper refused to budge on even the most minor privilege without formal permission from the council.

This household war was interrupted when Philip arrived from Spain in July of 1554. His father, Emperor Charles V, had instructed the dapper, blond prince to minimize his grandeur. Nevertheless, Philip came prancing into England with nine thousand noblemen and servants, one thousand mules and horses, and 3 million ducats in gold assembled in a fleet of 125 ships. Though most of his men were soldiers who remained aboard the ships, the exhibition of power was anything but modest; it made the English people feel all the more threatened. Twenty carts carried Philip's ninety-seven treasure chests to be guarded in the Tower of London. Some of his clothes were embroidered so heavily with gold that the color of the fabric was indiscernible.

Philip's mission was to keep England as Spain's ally, whatever happened. If

Queen Mary I, Elizabeth's half-sister, holding the rose that was the symbol of the Tudors. Mary became more grim and formidable as her reign proceeded. MANSELL COLLECTION.

Mary should die, either he or Elizabeth must inherit the throne to prevent its falling into the hands of the French-sympathizing Mary, Queen of Scots. Philip was therefore intent upon befriending Mary Tudor's sister. He asked Mary to bring Elizabeth, who had been prisoner at Woodstock for a year, to court. He planned to marry her off to some foreign Catholic prince, who would take her abroad and tame her.

Unlike Elizabeth, who had been born into scandal, Mary was a model of sexual virtue. No man had ever come near her. Now Philip, the pious Catholic with the fancy clothes and the grand manner, enchanted her. He did so reluctantly. Because of disease, poor sanitation, and generally harder living conditions, people aged more quickly than they do now. At thirty-seven, eleven years older than Philip, Mary was a tiny, melancholy woman with a deep, raspy voice, whose vivacity had been sapped by years of emotional turmoil. His father's advisers thought it necessary to tell him how to act: "For God's sake," one of them wrote, "appear to be pleased."

Philip married Mary for duty, hardly able to conceal his distaste for her, but she married him for love. Soon she announced that she was pregnant. She was aging and frail, and childbirth was dangerous for even the youngest, healthiest women. If Mary did not survive childbirth, Philip would face a crisis in England; he might even be killed. Mary submitted to Philip's wishes and called Elizabeth back to court, where her actions were closely watched. In the event of Mary's death, Elizabeth would be a hostage during the transition to Philip's regency. She seized the opportunity to charm Philip as she charmed so many other men throughout her life.

Mary's baby was expected in June. In August 1555, after a fitful, anxious summer, the queen still had produced no heir to the throne; her supposed pregnancy had been false. She may have had a tumor of the ovary, which caused the appearance of pregnancy. That there would be no child for Mary to love, and no heir to prevent Elizabeth's inheriting the kingdom, caused Mary devastating grief.

Exasperated and no longer able to put up with his clinging wife, the hostility of the English, or the expense of his stay with Mary, Philip left for the Hapsburg court in Brussels. Elizabeth withdrew to Hatfield and tried not to be noticed. Philip's father gave up the Hapsburg empire, turning over central Europe to his brother, Ferdinand I, and giving Spain, Naples, Sicily, the Netherlands, and colonies in the Americas to his son, Philip. Now King Philip II, Mary's husband had a throne of his own.

He did not return to England quickly, as he had promised, but remained in Brussels, conducting business and leading a wild life while Mary sat in a corner of her English palace and cried. She slapped Elizabeth with an ugly choice: either marry a Spanish duke or return to the Tower and die for disobedience.

Elizabeth had always taken pride in the fact that, while Catherine of Aragon's daughter was half Spanish, the daughter of Anne Boleyn was English through and through. She flatly refused to marry a foreigner. "The afflictions suffered by me are such that they have ridded me of any desire for a husband," she said. "I would rather die."

Mary dropped her threats when Elizabeth fell ill again. Spared for the time, Elizabeth nevertheless knew that her marriage and indeed her entire future were subject to another's whims. She must have felt like livestock.

When Philip returned to England after an absence of a year and a half, he came on business, not for love of Mary. He brought his mistress with him, an insult that must have pierced his wife, recalling Henry's abuse of Catherine of Aragon and Mary herself. Philip persuaded the queen to support the Spanish war against France. England held Calais, a fortress on the French coast, but relations with France were delicate. The Tudors had always played France and Spain against one another, avoiding alliances with either that would draw England into war. Having manipulated Mary in subordinating England's interests to Spain's, Philip departed abruptly. Mary removed his portrait from the council chamber; gossips said she had kicked it out of the room. She remarked to a friend that "God sent oft times to good women evil husbands."

Mary had never been trained for leadership. She had depended first on the Spanish ambassador for advice, then on Philip. Indeed, her Spanish husband had taken over the governance of England while he lived there; his name took precedence over Mary's in public documents, and he oversaw the administration of the English government. Although he was never crowned in England, people called him King Philip, and he acted the part. People argued publicly whether the laws of inheritance applied to Mary. A woman's wealth became her husband's legal property when she married; did a queen's realm transfer in the same way? It did in fact, if not by law, for Mary had lost her power to a husband who now had abandoned her.

In his absence, Philip left in charge the Catholic Cardinal Pole, an enemy of King Henry. The King had executed Pole's entire family; the cardinal's aged mother had been hacked to death by an incompetent axeman. The cardinal had lived in exile until Mary's reign had made England safe again for Catholics.

The Protestants were a vocal minority splintered into diverse sects, but Mary saw them as a unified threat, defiant to her rule and therefore dangerous. The Protestant Reformation of the Church had been in part a reaction to the abuse of religious power. A Counter Reformation ensued. Cardinal Pole had favored the revival in Europe of the medieval Inquisition, an official witch-hunt that enforced the laws of the Church with torture and execution. Now the actions of Mary's government more than compensated for her youthful denial of her faith. Who made the decision is unclear now, but in her name, Mary's government had begun in February 1555 to burn Protestants at the stake in Smithfield, a village on the outskirts of London.

The Church had tortured hundreds of thousands of Europeans for heresy, the denial of Roman Catholic beliefs. Philip himself once supervised a gigantic mass burning in Spain, where he told a victim who begged for mercy that he would burn his own son if the prince were a heretic. One inquisitor expressed the spirit of the Catholic Counter Reformation when he said, "It is no great matter whether they that die on account of religion be guilty or innocent, provided we terrify the people by such examples." The abstract goal of ridding society of the "ungodly" justified whatever personal wrongs occurred.

Compared with the Church's cruelties on the Continent, those of Mary's religious crusade were mild. But her purge was enough to earn her the name "Bloody Mary." Before the Smithfield Fires had been quenched, about three hundred

A Protestant being burned at the stake. All the Tudor governments committed such cruelties, but at Smithfield so many Protestants died in flames, accused of religious heresy during the reign of Queen Mary I, that their deaths became known as "the Smithfield Fires." BY PERMISSION OF THE BRITISH LIBRARY.

Protestants, including some sixty women, had died in flames during Mary's four-year reign. (Henry VIII had burned eighty-one in thirty-eight years. Five people burned at the stake in Elizabeth's forty-five years on the throne.) Most of the Smithfield martyrs were humble folk who could neither escape to Europe nor temper their opposition to Mary's religious laws. The executioners were often inept, building the fires with wet wood and rushes that burned slowly. One man sang hymns until his lips were burned away. As she burned, a woman gave birth; the executioners threw the baby back into the fire. The agony was so extreme that people tied bags of gunpowder at the crotches, necks, and underarms of condemned loved ones, hoping that the fire would kill them quickly by explosion rather than scorch them slowly.

Of course, more and more of Mary's people hated her as more and more of them died. Protestants had once seemed like mere noisy troublemakers. The cruelty made them martyrs. "Be of good comfort, and play the man," one Protestant cleric said prophetically to another as the flames licked their hands and faces. "We shall this day light such a candle, by God's grace, in England, as I trust shall never be put out." The burnings became associated with foreign ideas, especially Catholicism.

Religion was not the only strain on the country. Philip's war in France went badly. Before the conflict ended, Calais had fallen, a loss that was an appalling blow to Mary's reputation. She never recovered from her shame.

In the meantime, the Elizabethan Age was about to dawn, for Mary, ill with what was probably cancer, was dying. As her health declined, the number of visitors to Elizabeth at Hatfield steadily grew. Her household sparkled with gaiety in contrast to Mary's melancholy court. Even Mary's own courtiers traveled to Elizabeth's palace, positioning themselves for the transfer of power they knew was coming.

The queen agreed at last not to obstruct Elizabeth's claim to the throne if she would promise to pay Mary's debts and maintain the Catholic Church. Elizabeth solemnly promised, but she must have laughed behind the queen's back, for nobody except Mary expected the Protestant princess to support Catholicism.

Experience as Queen Mary's subject had taught Elizabeth lessons she never forgot. She later said she had learned how to keep silent, and discovered what "practices" go on behind a monarch's back; she suggested that she had heard more than one plan to depose Mary. That experience would make her leery of naming a successor when she herself was monarch, lest conspirators revolt against her in turn. From her imprisonment in the Tower she had learned compassion for those caught in the whirlpool of royal intrigue. And the people, whose affection for Elizabeth restrained Mary's vengeance, had taught her the power of their sympathetic support.

On November 17, 1558, Mary Tudor died. Four hours later, Cardinal Pole also died of natural causes. Several councilors hurried with the news to Hatfield. There, according to legend, the twenty-five-year-old Elizabeth was reading a Greek Bible under an oak tree when a horseman galloped up, carrying Mary Tudor's ring as proof of her death. Elizabeth was not surprised to learn that she was now queen. She closed her book and fell to her knees. "Time has brought us to this place," she said. "This is the Lord's doing, and it is marvelous in our eyes."

7

THE NEW QUEEN CROWNED

By noon on November 17, 1558, the day of Mary's death at the age of forty-two, Elizabeth had been officially declared Queen of England, the fourth monarch in the twelve years since Henry's death. A writer said of the realm Elizabeth was inheriting: "I never saw England weaker in strength, men, money and riches. . . . Here was nothing but fining, beheading, hanging, quartering and burning; taxing, levying, pulling down of bulwarks at home; and beggaring and losing our stronghold abroad. . . . A few priests . . . ruled all." Mary had felt so endangered by the people's hostility that, by the end of her life, she had increased her troop of bodyguards from the fifty men of Henry's time to five hundred.

With the death of Mary Tudor, the Spanish King Philip lost his power over the English people; the persecution of Protestants ended, and those who had fled could return home. Londoners sang and danced in the streets until exhaustion forced them home to bed.

Whatever the merriment in London, however, the work of the new reign, begun long before Mary died, intensified at the new queen's palace in Hatfield. Without delay Elizabeth had to form a new government, loyal to her rather than to the memory of her Catholic sister. The new queen immediately named William Cecil her secretary of state. Her servant since 1550, Cecil was a Protestant who dressed in sober black amid the gold-embroidered dandies of the court. It may have been he who had warned Elizabeth and Mary of danger when Edward died. He had been discreet enough in his religion to hold a minor position in Mary's government, but he recorded in his journal the name of every Protestant she killed for heresy.

William Cecil, Lord Burghley, Elizabeth's secretary of state and later her treasurer, helped her establish a government and served her the rest of his days.
Bodleian Library.

A man as sly and ambitious as Elizabeth had learned to be, Cecil came to understand her unpredictability and deceit as no one else ever would. He became her reliable comrade, responsible for her government's foreign policy and the secret service. He also kept track of events throughout England and intercepted trouble before it began. He would serve Elizabeth and the realm tirelessly for some forty years.

Cecil was not the only person whose loyalty the new queen had to enlist. On the day after Mary's death, Elizabeth held her first meeting with her privy council. While she dismissed two-thirds of Mary's councilors, including the Catholic priests, ten men stayed on, for Elizabeth knew that she needed experienced advisers for the sake of stability and a smooth transition. Drawing from as wide a pool as possible, she appointed noblemen, courtiers, lawyers, and businessmen. Some had served Edward, and two had participated in the Wyatt Rebellion. Cecil, thirteen years older than the twenty-five-year-old Elizabeth, was the youngest councilor; most were over fifty. In filling other positions, she rewarded friends. Kate Ashley became mistress of the maids of honor, and Elizabeth appointed her childhood friend Robert Dudley master of the horse. She had clearly forgiven him his part in his family's attempted coup.

While the council were all men, women were the queen's companions and servants in her living quarters. Attending Elizabeth's physical and emotional needs, their very intimacy made them dangerous, as biographer Carolly Erickson observes. The ladies of the chamber dished up the queen's food and cleaned her clothes, service that would have enabled them to poison her. The cook knew whether she was too sick to eat. The laundress knew her menstrual cycle, and therefore could cast light on her physical health; she would know whether the queen was pregnant and when menopause had ended the possibility of royal heirs. Elizabeth's waiting women would witness her love affairs and overhear her most personal conversations and quarrels.

Elizabeth could not be surrounded night and day in her bedroom and at her dining table by Mary's personal friends, who were all too likely to spy and sell information to Spain and France, the pope, and even the queen's own courtiers. She dismissed every one of Mary's ladies, replacing them with her own relatives and friends. She forbade them to discuss politics with her. Consequently, since they had no favors to dispense, they lacked the personal power of male courtiers who were known to have the queen's ear.

On November 23 Elizabeth Tudor rode into London accompanied by one thousand men and women. Once again, she showed her awareness that *seeming* power was essential to *actual* power. Officials welcomed her. She allowed them to kiss her hand until she saw the approach of London's Bishop Bonner, the fearsome persecutor of Protestants during Mary's reign. She withdrew her hand abruptly and avoided him.

Mary was buried without a monument at Westminster Abbey nearly a month after her death. To this day, she has no monument. In his funeral sermon for Mary, the Catholic Bishop of Winchester said, "I praise the dead more than the living." He went on to observe that the English would have to obey their new queen, since "a living dog is better than a dead lion." Displaying remarkable restraint in the face of these words, Elizabeth merely confined the bishop to his house for a month.

On the advice of a respected astrologer, John Dee, Elizabeth and the privy council planned the coronation for January 15, 1559. Everyone in the royal household was fitted out with new clothing. The laundress received a new red dress. The fools, whose job was to amuse the queen, would wear orange velvet with purple tinsel. As Mary had lain dying, the ladies of London had been buying the fabrics for their coronation gowns. Some had sent to Brussels, where the finest silks and velvets were made. The privy council stopped the unloading of crimson silk from ships until Elizabeth had chosen the cloth she wanted "for the furniture of her coronation."

The ceremonies were as splendid as the clothing. Robert Dudley, who as master of the horse planned the court's great rituals and constantly attended the queen, probably organized the elaborate spectacle. After spending a night or two at the Tower, according to custom, Elizabeth rode in a procession past the decorated houses of London. Several days of drizzle had left the unpaved streets a wallow of mud and slush and deep puddles. Workmen filled the worst holes and scattered fresh gravel on the streets so that the parade would not be mired down.

Matched mules carried Elizabeth's litter, which was covered with gold brocade, and Robert Dudley followed on a magnificent horse, leading her own favorite horse by the reins. The queen wore a cloth-of-gold gown and an ermine cloak. Her red-coated company of bodyguards surrounded her, armed and on foot. The procession of one thousand horses took more than an hour to pass. People whose houses overlooked the route had invited guests or sold places in the windows.

In neighborhood after neighborhood Elizabeth's subjects performed pageants for her honor and entertainment. She repeatedly stopped the parade to listen and praise the performers. Everywhere choirs and speeches and crowds honored the queen. She received flowers from the people's hands and kept at her side all day a bouquet of fragrant rosemary, a gift from a poor woman. She permitted individuals to approach and give her their blessings.

The beginnings of Elizabeth's image as Good Queen Bess, the monarch devoted to her subjects, were already evident. She knew that she owed her own survival to the love of her people, and that her government would thrive only with their goodwill. They were watching every move she made. Self-interest dictated that throughout the rest of her life, she act in such a way as to dramatize her connection with them. Beyond selfishness, she had a genuine sense of God-anointed duty to *their* best interest.

When a city official gave her a crimson purse filled with gold coins, she replied with a pretty speech: "Be ye assured that I will be as good unto you as ever Queen was to her people. No will in me can lack, neither do I trust shall there lack any power. And persuade yourselves, that for the safety and quietness of you all, I will not spare if need be to spend my blood."

The next day, Elizabeth was crowned Queen of England, wearing a cloth-of-gold gown and a cape made of crimson velvet lined with ermine. Her gold crown was set atop a crimson velvet cap embroidered in gold and pearls. Her long red hair hung down around her shoulders, in the style of maidens at their marriages. The ostentatious clothing was uncomfortable and very heavy, but, as Lacey Baldwin Smith observes, it was necessary to Elizabeth's position. Her power lay in a blend of tyranny, intimidation, and charm. Her clothes were a working uniform, a visible symbol of her power and authority, rather like a general's insignias, medals, and gold braid.

Elizabeth had continued to hear Mass with her household every day and had forbidden attacks on religious places and persons. During a Mass in her private chapel in December, however, she had chastised a bishop when he elevated the host for adoration. Protestants rejected the Roman Catholic belief that the bread and wine of the sacrament were transformed into the literal flesh and blood of Christ; they took communion as a remembrance of Jesus's sacrifice. When the bishop defiantly lifted the host all the higher, Elizabeth stormed out of the chapel. That very week she ordered that church services everywhere be conducted in English.

A coronation was a religious ceremony as well as a political one. As a result of this scandal, one bishop after another refused to put the crown on Elizabeth's Protestant head. The reluctant bishop who was persuaded at last conducted the

Mass in Latin, according to the Catholic rites. But the queen did not take the sacrament and, at her command, he administered the oath by reading from an English Bible that William Cecil held. As the bishop anointed the headstrong Elizabeth with holy oil, she growled, "Thy ointment stinks."

The compromise made the ceremony awkward but tolerable to all the parties. At last the crowned queen emerged from Westminster Abbey wearing a purple velvet mantle, so exuberant that an Italian diplomat wrote to his government about her insufficient dignity. Souvenir hunters cut up seven hundred yards of magnificent blue carpet on which she had trod.

By now, having traveled for days through the muddy streets of London in the January chill, Elizabeth had caught cold. Nevertheless, she attended the banquet that culminated the ceremonies. According to ancient tradition, a horseman, the queen's champion, rode into the hall on a great warhorse, flung down his gauntlet, and challenged anyone who "should deny her to be the righteous and lawful queen of this realm." At last she went home to bed, while the banquet continued until one o'clock in the morning.

The magnificent ceremonies surrounding Elizabeth's accession to the throne were enormously expensive, and Queen Mary had left the government worse than broke, staggering under debt. Nevertheless, seizing the opportunity for a spectacle, Elizabeth spent more than sixteen thousand pounds on her coronation, at a time when a man in Dudley's service earned fifty pounds in a year; a little more than two pounds annually was deemed an adequate income for a common man. She knew that she would gain and keep power only if she looked powerful. The pomp and grandeur of her coronation suggested the second theme of her reign. In addition to the role of Good Queen Bess, she was theatrically establishing her identity as the goddess Gloriana. The splendor of that mask set her in the public mind above the tumult of real life, and even beyond reproach. The combined images were masterly propaganda, manipulated with cunning.

An observer of the ceremonies noticed Elizabeth's aptness for the role her country required of her:

> If ever any person had either the gift or the style to win
> the hearts of the people, it was their Queen. All her
> faculties were in motion and every motion seemed well
> guided action: her eye was set upon one, her ear listened
> to another, her judgment ran upon a third, to a fourth she
> addressed her speech; her spirit seemed to be every-
> where and yet so entire in herself, as it seemed to be
> nowhere else.

The queen had begun the long romance with her people that accounted in part for the spectacular success of her reign.

8
THE NEW QUEEN IN CHARGE

ELIZABETH'S INTEREST IN HER GOVERNMENT surprised her officials, but she would need more than interest to bring the realm through the crisis she had inherited. One official summarized the problems she faced: "The Queen poor, the realm exhausted, the nobility poor and decayed. Want of good captains and soldiers. The people out of order. Justice not executed. All things dear [expensive]. Excess in meat, drink and apparel. Divisions among ourselves. Wars with France and Scotland. . . . Steadfast enmity but no steadfast friendship abroad." Circumstances limited Elizabeth's options. She was bound by traditions and institutions that had evolved over centuries. An envoy was arranging a foreign loan from the Netherlands to relieve the poverty that further blocked her.

The English yearned for order and stability; for them, any change suggested corruption and impending disaster. England had undergone some thirty years of devastating shocks. The people had been jolted from one religion to another, back again, and yet again. Foreigners had dragged them into war. Twice rebels had

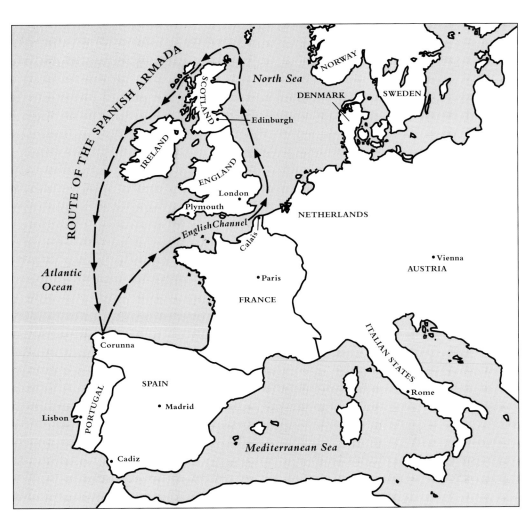

A map of sixteenth-century Europe.

tried to overthrow the God-anointed monarchy. Now another Protestant monarch, the daughter of a disreputable woman, had come to power. Modern people, accustomed to continuous and accelerating technological change and the systematic change of governments after elections, can hardly imagine the shock these sudden shifts must have caused in the sixteenth century. The English people were dizzy with the disruption of their old customs.

In addition to the shortage of money, Elizabeth's government faced two gigantic problems immediately: religious conflict and the threat of invasion. The hostility between Catholics and Protestants was an emergency. Would Elizabeth return the country to King Edward's religious position or Mary's? Nobody knew the queen's intentions, and the people had to see what was demanded of them before they could accept the latest changes; otherwise friction would destroy the realm. Many people feared religious civil war.

Related to the religious issue was the danger of invasion from the north. Hostile French soldiers were gathered just across the northern border, supporting the Scottish government. And the Catholic Mary, Queen of Scots claimed that she was the rightful Queen of England as well.

At the beginning of Elizabeth's reign, all of Europe was embroiled in conflict. Peace negotiations were ending the political struggle that had entangled France and Spain for decades. But the religious struggle was just beginning. Henry's new church had unbalanced compromises that had evolved over centuries. Catholicism's customary power had been transferred to the state. Politics throughout Europe had polarized along religious lines; Catholic and Protestant factions struggled to determine which side would control the future.

In the face of this turmoil, Elizabeth was a novice leader who had to *win* the respect of legal courts, Parliament, and council. Though later she would back away, she began by attending meetings of the privy council, determined to govern her elders and to dominate them through knowledge of the realm's affairs. Nor did she embroider handkerchiefs during these meetings, as Mary Stuart was later said to do in Scotland.

At council meetings Elizabeth controlled her councilors, men more experienced than she, by being unpredictable and temperamental. They were kept off balance by her acid humor; no one knew what she might say next. Elizabeth listened, sometimes making scathing remarks about the proceedings, and then she

QUEEN ELIZABETH I'S
LIFE IN PORTRAITS

Princess Elizabeth at the age of perhaps fourteen, displaying her beautiful hands, with the books that were her companions throughout her life. BY KIND PERMISSION OF HER MAJESTY QUEEN ELIZABETH II.

The Coronation Portrait. The Virgin Queen, at twenty-five years of age, wears her hair down over her shoulders like a bride, holding the symbols of her majesty, the ruler's orb and scepter.
NATIONAL PORTRAIT GALLERY, LONDON.

The Rainbow Portrait. The goddess Gloriana, a glamorized image of Elizabeth I, holds the rainbow in her hand as if she were herself the source of light. The serpent embroidered on her sleeve symbolizes wisdom; the eyes and ears that decorate her robe suggest that she is all-seeing, all-hearing, all-knowing. FOTOMAS, BY KIND PERMISSION OF THE MARQUESS OF SALISBURY.

The Ermine Portrait. An ermine perches on the Virgin Queen's sleeve; the animal's whiteness symbolizes purity of heart and chastity. Gold embroidery and enormous rubies and other jewels embellish her gown, and she wears a triple rope of rare black pearls. FOTOMAS, BY KIND PERMISSION OF THE MARQUESS OF SALISBURY.

The Feather Fan Portrait. Good Queen Bess looks very prim and proper. Her image bristles with intelligence and formidable personality, however, leaving no doubt that she is in charge. NATIONAL PORTRAIT GALLERY, LONDON.

The Armada Portrait. Windows in the background open onto two phases of the battle against the Spanish Armada of 1587: the Armada on its way and the storm heaven-sent to aid the English fleet. At age fifty-four Elizabeth holds the world under her right hand. BY KIND PERMISSION OF THE MARQUESS OF TAVISTOCK AND THE TRUSTEES OF THE BEDFORD ESTATE.

The Ditchley portrait of Elizabeth I, painted in 1592 when the queen was nearly sixty years old, portrays her standing astride a map of England, leading her realm into clear weather after a storm. NATIONAL PORTRAIT GALLERY, LONDON.

announced her wishes, leaving no room for argument. She who had always been imperious acted like a king from the start.

She also took an interest in the mail. In Cecil's view, the queen's meddling in practical affairs was a pesky intrusion on his privileges by a woman, a creature supposed to be naturally inferior even though she was a queen. Having worked for the volatile Mary, Cecil distrusted women's judgment, a view that his fellows on the council shared. When a messenger took a letter directly to Elizabeth, Cecil scolded him, calling "a matter of such weight . . . too much for a woman's knowledge."

The Count of Feria, the new Spanish ambassador, was also bewildered by the queen's presumption. Not only was she "a young lass who, although sharp, is without prudence," he wrote King Philip, her impetuosity was all the more dangerous because she was "incomparably more feared than her sister, and gives her orders and has her way as absolutely as her father did." Mary had shouted at her council, but they ignored her. Men were not accustomed to obeying orders from strong-minded women; they expected deference and dependency. Moreover, Elizabeth lacked a proper reverence for him, the ambassador said, and seemed to read his secret thoughts and poke fun at them. "She is a very strange sort of woman," he advised his sponsors.

Though she was queen, Elizabeth's power was not absolute. Even her father, the great Henry, had felt obliged to make his annulments and remarriages at least *seem* legal. Elizabeth's life depended upon the people's approval; indeed, not many decades after her death, Puritan rebels would kill the English king. And her policies' success with the people depended upon the cooperation of her officials, who could sabotage them if they wished.

She kept a tight rein on her secretaries, overworking them and refusing to allow them to hire assistants, which would have blurred responsibility and placed another layer of authority between herself and her people. She took all the credit for her government's achievements but blamed her officials mercilessly when policies failed. She paid stingy wages, but she honored the councilors at court, found high positions for them, took an interest in their families, visited them, and gave them rich gifts of lands, exclusive licenses to sell goods, and personal baubles.

Everyone who spoke to the queen did so on bended knee. It was a great honor when she offered her hand and invited a person to stand in a conversation with her. She was the center of attention wherever she went. Her privy chamber was a private sitting room, where others came only by invitation. Beyond was the presence chamber, where courtiers congregated. Then came the guard or watching chamber, a semipublic place, and then the great hall. The outer rooms were crowded with sightseers and petitioners who had come to ask favors.

She ruled as she lived, selfishly, with a highly personal policy and style. Her courtiers were expected to sacrifice their own personal interests for hers, even to forgo marriage for service to the queen.

Government ministers and chambermaids alike learned to watch her mood; those who had already met with her advised the others whether the time was right to present a problem. Her secretary and other councilors hurried away with papers she had signed, before she could change her mind. They learned to request her orders in writing so she could not deny them after they had obeyed her. They bantered with her to distract her attention when they wanted her signature, hoping that she wouldn't rewrite the document or refuse to sign it at all.

Her unpredictability exasperated the councilors but also prevented their running away with her power. She was such an artist at deception, so "full of words" and so "apt to lie" that it was almost impossible to know exactly her intentions. What her impatient servants did not notice was that her indecision and secrecy protected her position. Delay was a deliberate tactic to control her friends and confound her enemies, preventing their preparations for murder or other plots. With delays, she also avoided rash action and waited for conflicts to sort themselves out.

Wherever Elizabeth went, a crowd of people followed. Here a courtier kneels before the queen, while attendants serve a hunting picnic from barrels of wine and a hamper of roasted fowl, hams, and ribs. MANSELL COLLECTION.

Elizabeth rewarded people who had made trouble during the previous reign. Riding through London, she glimpsed one of Mary Tudor's Protestant enemies in a window and called out a warm greeting to him. He who had been most traitorous, the Spanish ambassador reported, was "best thought of." To make matters

worse, the queen permitted sacrilege at court. In one holiday play, actors cos-
tumed as wolves and crows and asses wore the robes of Catholic abbots, cardinals,
and bishops.

While the Protestants were only a small minority in England, many of them
lived in London, and pressure from them was loud. They had put their hope in
Elizabeth as their savior since King Edward's death. Their joy at her accession
arose from their expectation that she would forcefully advance the Reformation.

She had no such intention. She enjoyed the beauty and spectacle of old religious ceremonies, the rituals and vestments, the comfortable regularity. Both candles and crucifix stood on the altar in her private chapel. She wanted an altar,
tapestries, and intricately carved stone and wood, not the table and plain painted
walls of the Puritans. The idea of married parsons disgusted her. She wanted
common people to accept unchanging beliefs handed down from the top, not to
rebel by interpreting the Bible to suit themselves.

Although she said that bishops were "lazy poltroons," she passionately
believed in hierarchy. Like Henry, Elizabeth had no doubt that the English
church and its commoners required a head, merely disputing whether it should
be the pope or herself. But as queen of all the English people, she was determined to navigate a middle way between the radical Catholics and the extremist
Puritans. As she did with most things, she waffled and hesitated, using the tactics of cunning delay, to ride out the turbulence until the furor should settle and
the conflict fade away.

The people forced the issue, however. At the end of January Elizabeth opened
her first Parliament, a meeting of the two bodies that represented the nobility and
the common people. They met irregularly, as the need arose. Members of the
House of Commons represented the gentry and ordinary folk, while the upper
body, the House of Lords, were noblemen and clergy. Beautifully dressed again in
gold and crimson, ermine and pearls, Elizabeth attended the Mass that custom-

arily opened a session of Parliament, but, when she saw a procession of monks, she upbraided them. "Away with those torches, for we see very well," she snapped.

Parliament was an irksome formality, Elizabeth felt. As God's representative on earth, she was divinely inspired. Throughout her reign she cited her God-given superiority. "If I were not persuaded that mine were the true way of God's will," she said once, "God forbid I should live to prescribe it to you." Her divinity enabled her to make decisions; monarchs had "a princely understanding such as private persons cannot have." The House of Lords was there, she thought, to approve her judgment and create laws to carry it out. It was the role of the House of Commons to vote for taxes and raise the money she required.

In Elizabeth's view Parliament's job was to do her bidding. Its members saw their role as something more substantial. The monarch could collect money only with their agreement, which they could withhold if the government's actions displeased them. They increasingly proposed new laws, and they used the power of the purse to pressure the ruler to act as they thought best.

The Catholic bishops refused to cooperate with Elizabeth's wish to return the English church to its condition at the time of Henry's death; they resigned their positions as a group. The Bishop of Winchester cited the authority of St. Paul, that no female could act as apostle, shepherd, doctor, or preacher, and Parliament balked at naming a woman Supreme Head of the Church of England. Elizabeth compromised and accepted the title of Supreme Governor.

Puritans, the most radical Protestants in Parliament, pressed for radical changes in doctrine. (It was the Puritans who would later flee to the Netherlands, then establish a "community of saints" in the American wilderness.) The queen compromised again, accepting the Book of Common Prayer that King Edward had introduced but adding a sentence to the Protestant statement of the sacrament that would satisfy Catholics. The church kept the beautiful robes and other trappings repulsive to the Puritans, who called them the "livery of the Anti-Christ."

Queen Elizabeth I, flanked by officials of her government, sitting in Parliament before the House of Commons, Bishops of the Church of England, noblemen, judges, and others of high rank.
HULTON GETTY.

Before Henry VIII's time, nobody could own a Bible without a license, for ordinary people were not considered competent to understand it. Protestants wanted every plowboy to be as familiar with scripture as a priest, but traditionalists thought that such knowledge would encourage the questioning of authority. In 1530, before Henry proclaimed the English church independent of Rome, to own or read an English Bible was a criminal offense, punishable by burning at the stake. During Elizabeth's reign, however, Bible reading became almost universal.

At the same time, attendance at Catholic Mass was made a crime punishable by life imprisonment if a person repeated the offense three times, but in practice this law would be elastic and loosely enforced. Elizabeth knew, she said, "what it is to be a subject," and she had no intention of "making windows into men's souls." Roman Catholics would practice underground religion. Puritans would agitate for further change. But after the blood of Mary's reign, Elizabeth's religious compromise was a settlement that England preferred to open warfare or the burning of heretics.

By delaying extreme religious reforms, moreover, Elizabeth put off her own excommunication from the Church, which would have exposed England to attack by any monarch determined to replace her with a Catholic queen. The likeliest prospect for her crown was Mary, Queen of Scots. In the eyes of Catholic Europe, those who had never accepted Henry's remarriages, she had a better right to England's throne than Elizabeth.

The French political support for the Scottish queen could result in a military attack from the outside, while Catholics within England always threatened rebellion. Thus Elizabeth's position was doubly dangerous. And England was caught between the pincers of Spain and France, each nation wanting alliance with England to fend off the threat of the other. These pressures necessitated a delicate dance that would require all the deception Elizabeth had mastered during Mary Tudor's reign. Her government would therefore encourage hostilities between

England's two powerful neighbors across the Channel, always dangling before them the lure of English friendship without being dominated or drawn into a war.

As Elizabeth's reign began, her diplomats were attending peace talks in Calais, the territory Mary had lost when Philip involved England in Spain's continual war with France. In fact, peace papers had been sent for Mary's signature when she was on her deathbed, too ill even to read. These documents had been lost in the confusion: The oblivious morticians had used the long scrolls to wrap Mary's body! Negotiations with the French continued with new copies of the papers.

At least France and Spain lay across the Channel; an attack from there could come only from the sea. But the army of Catholic Scotland, reinforced by French soldiers, gathered strength. Elizabeth began to buy arms and other war matériel and to build up her fortresses on the Scottish border. The danger became urgent when a faction of Protestant noblemen and gentlemen in Scotland, who called themselves the Lords of the Congregation, raised an armed rebellion against the Catholic government of Scotland. This government ruled the country for Mary, who had lived in France since being sent there in childhood to be educated in the royal court.

Mary's father, King James V of Scotland, had married the French Mary of Guise. When he died only six days after his daughter Mary's birth, the infant's mother had become regent and had ruled Scotland ever since. The Protestant revolutionaries opposed the regent's foreign attachments and favored religious reform. They begged for English help.

Before she had grown into her crown, Elizabeth faced a thorny choice. As in the countries on the Continent, the pressure for religious change was associated with political rebellion. If Elizabeth refused assistance to the Scottish rebels, the threat of the French army would remain at England's very door; the Protestant cause and the expulsion of foreigners from Scotland were in the interest of England. If Elizabeth provided assistance, however, she would break her dearest principle, openly joining a treasonous rabble against a lawful crown.

Elizabeth's own self-interest was at the heart of that principle. Mary was Scotland's queen by divine right; it was "against God's law to aid any subjects against their natural princes or their ministers," Elizabeth firmly believed. If England could aid a rebellion against Mary, Queen of Scots, then Scotland—or France, Spain, Austria, or any other power-hungry monarchy—could do likewise to the Queen of England herself. England's intervention in Scottish affairs might even cause a French invasion of Scotland.

Nevertheless, Cecil urged sending assistance to the Lords of the Congregation. It was a rare opportunity for a new union of interests between England and Scotland, and the queen's own safety made her help imperative. Cecil's policy won over Elizabeth's reluctance to meddle in another queen's realm, and her commitment grew little by little until England was involved on both land and sea.

Cecil went to Scotland to negotiate the withdrawal of the French troops. Almost immediately, in June 1560, Mary's mother died. Storms and English blockades headed off the French fleet that might have brought aid to Scotland. And religious war exploded in France between the Catholics and the Protestants, compelling the government to focus on its own internal problems. The Scottish rebels set up a Protestant state, and Mary's illegitimate half-brother, the Earl of Moray, took control.

Despite Cecil's spectacular success, he returned to a cold queen who offered him no praise or gratitude. In his absence Robert Dudley had influenced Elizabeth against him. Cecil had, after all, persuaded her against her will to sponsor an uprising of foreign Protestants, which made her seem all the more a menace to the European Catholic states. Moreover, control of events had shifted from Elizabeth to military leaders distant from court, a situation she would always abhor. The older, more experienced Cecil had manipulated the council to favor his plans and had seized the reins from Elizabeth.

She must take them back.

9

"THE QUEEN'S A WOMAN!"

URING THE SIXTEENTH CENTURY, death was everybody's companion. What modern people think minor crimes were capital offenses to the Elizabethans. Death from accidents, tuberculosis, pneumonia, bubonic plague, sweating sickness, or smallpox happened every day. Nobody knew what caused disease, let alone how to cure it; bacteria, viruses, antibiotics, and anesthesia had not yet been discovered. Writers expressed the people's wry pessimism with the Latin phrase *carpe diem*—seize the day. Anything might happen, and suddenly, without warning; one must live life fully while one could.

In addition to the hazards everybody suffered, most women of Elizabeth's time experienced biological servitude, giving birth to as many as twelve children or even more between their mid teens and their late thirties, if indeed they survived childbirth at all. Parents expected that many of their children would die; the loss was an inescapable fact of life. It is no wonder that women were thought weak, since they were perpetually pregnant or recovering from childbirth. Fathers had legal control of their children as a matter of course, as they controlled what had formerly been their wives' money; if a woman left her husband, she had to leave her children and everything else she had.

Lacking a secure succession, the kingdom was haunted by the possibility of the queen's death. In addition, the potential heirs to England's throne were all female. Though she might die in childbirth, the risk was her duty as woman and queen. Elizabeth needed a husband. As long as she remained childless, the succession could be disputed, and the realm would be vulnerable to attack. England needed a Protestant heir—male, of course.

It is not surprising, therefore, that Elizabeth's first Parliament in 1559 demanded to talk about her marriage before speaking of other business. Parliament had a rightful interest in the matter. If Elizabeth should die without an heir, the nation would likely plunge into civil war. Some members of Parliament were Protestants whose lives would be in danger if she were deposed in favor of a Catholic ruler.

Elizabeth replied forcefully to Parliament's request. She had always preferred to remain single; now that she bore the heavy duties of government, marriage would be an "inconsiderate folly" that would only distract her from her work. She dramatically removed her coronation ring from her finger and flashed it before the members' eyes. She already had a husband—England. "Behold . . . the Pledge of this my Wedlock and Marriage with my Kingdom," she said. "Every one of you, and as many as are English-men, are Children and Kinsmen to me."

Though she listened politely to the fears of Parliament, Elizabeth did not give an inch, refusing even to admit that her marriage was its concern. In her formal speech to the House of Commons, she said that whether she married was her own business and she did not appreciate parliamentary interference. She had always resisted Mary's attempts to force a husband on her, she said, even under threat of death, and she would not change now. She preferred to leave the matter to Providence, but she would be content if her tombstone read "a Queen, having reigned such a time, lived and died a virgin."

As always when his own interests were concerned, King Philip was willing to help. "It would be better for herself and her kingdom," he wrote, "if she would take a consort who might relieve her of those labors which are only fit for men." He volunteered for the job in January 1559, before Elizabeth was crowned, offering to do his duty for the sake of European stability. "I have decided," he said grandly, "to place on one side all other considerations which might be urged against it, and am resolved to render this service to God and offer to marry the Queen of England." He would do so, however, only if she became a Catholic and agreed to uphold the faith as Philip saw fit. "In this way it will be evident and manifest that I am serving the Lord in marrying her and that she had been converted by my act."

Elizabeth's betrothal to Philip had been considered when she was only a baby. After his marriage to Mary he had incessantly tried to marry off Elizabeth to one Spanish aristocrat or another to assure her continued friendship toward his country; marriage would also have silenced her and taken her out of England, where, as heir, she had irritated Mary Tudor's suspicions. Now Philip was offering himself as husband to his dead wife's sister. Elizabeth surely noticed that he was proposing the very kind of suspect marriage between in-laws that Henry had used as an excuse for dissolving his marriage to Catherine of Aragon. Of course Elizabeth refused to adopt Philip's religion, which saved her further explanation, but she might well have laughed at his presumption.

Soon Philip was betrothed to a thirteen-year-old French princess; that marriage would make him brother-in-law to Mary, Queen of Scots. The age of his bride was not unusual. During the Renaissance, the average age of girls at marriage was fourteen to sixteen; boys were between the ages of eighteen and twenty-one. Farm people tended to marry younger, as did those of the upper class, whose weddings were business arrangements to unify large estates; the largest estates anywhere were royal kingdoms.

During the 1559 jousting tournament to celebrate Philip's betrothal, a lance shattered, and a splinter of wood pierced the eye of the French King Henry II. He died a few days later. His son took the throne at the age of fourteen, and the wife of the new King Francis II, the fifteen-year-old Mary, Queen of Scots, became the Queen of France as well as Scotland. The marriage had been arranged when he was five months old and she two years. The royal couple lived in France, where Mary's French uncles governed for the young king. They refused to ratify the peace treaty England had negotiated with Scotland. The peril Mary posed for Elizabeth's reign became ever more obvious.

Elizabeth must have been insulted by Philip's belief that she needed his masculine assistance to govern, but the attitude he expressed was universal. The contempt for women was a second reason, in addition to the lack of an heir, for Parliament's insistence that Elizabeth promise to marry. Such assumptions were expressed indirectly in a dispatch to the Hapsburg Emperor Ferdinand I from his ambassador, who thought that one of the imperial archdukes should marry Elizabeth and "rule her and England."

Once as Elizabeth rode through the streets of London, a woman who evidently saw her nearby for the first time swooned. "My God, the Queen's a woman!" she gasped as she collapsed and fainted. She was shocked that Elizabeth was not a goddess, after all, but a mere mortal female.

Everyone "knew" that Elizabeth's femininity disqualified her for the position of ruler, for, as one contemporary writer said, "every woman would willingly be a man, as every deformed wretch, a goodly and fair creature; and every idiot and fool, learned and wise." Roger Ascham, her admiring teacher, had praised her because he thought her virtues distinguished her from other women: "The constitution of her mind is exempt from female weakness and she is endued with a masculine power of application." Even her tomb now reminds us that she had "excellent adornments both of body and mind, and excellent . . . princely virtues beyond her sex."

John Knox, a Protestant leader in Scotland, was horrified by the very idea of women having such power as Elizabeth now held over men, a condition he considered monstrous and contrary to God's laws. During Mary Tudor's reign, he had attacked her; Mary, Queen of Scots; and the Scottish Mary's mother, Mary of Guise. He had urged the assassination of these Catholic queens. The dogs, he predicted, would drink the Scottish Mary's blood. Knox's pamphlet, *First Blast of the Trumpet Against the Monstrous Regiment* [government] *of Women,* was a tirade.

Knox's ideas infuriated Elizabeth. Her rage worried him, for he wanted England to support the Protestant regime in Scotland. Therefore he moderated his extreme views in a letter to Cecil. Elizabeth was a blessed exception to the natural law, Knox wrote, a woman whom God had appointed the savior of her country. Although "both nature and God's law doth deny to all women" equality with men, Knox could support Elizabeth's authority if she confessed that her power was a special dispensation by God, something supernatural and not to be extended to other women.

Apart from the slander against her gender, the queen never approved of any rebels' disobedience to lawful authority, and Knox had defied the crown of Scotland. Elizabeth was not pacified by his arrogant apology. She was certainly not a feminist in the modern sense of the word, but she had seen what had happened to Mary Tudor. Though Mary had continued to work at her desk from dawn to dark, her real authority had flowed to Philip through the wedding ring she wore on her finger. Spain had gained such power in the English government that the privy council that confirmed Elizabeth's own right to the throne was presided over by the Spanish ambassador representing the king of Spain. The young queen did not intend to repeat her sister's mistake.

There was no shortage of applicants for the position of Elizabeth's bridegroom, but few of them were English. None of the queen's countrymen was a prince with royal blood, and the only duke by birth was Norfolk, who already had a wife. (He was the son of the Duke of Norfolk who had bullied Mary Tudor.) But the Protestant King of Sweden and Catholic kings and archdukes sent their emissaries to pay Elizabeth court. She enjoyed their flattery and led them on, as if she were playing chess.

On the one side, a king could not make a direct proposal of marriage, for his image could not stand a refusal. On the other, Elizabeth's marriageable status was one of her greatest treasures, for it enabled her to dangle the possibility of an English throne before the monarchs of Europe, keeping potential enemies off balance by making them think an alliance might be near. It was a game she would play for decades with exquisite finesse. She let her advisers think she was seriously trying to choose a royal husband. In fact, however, she was infatuated with her master of the horse, Robert Dudley.

Their childhood acquaintance was only part of what they had in common. At different times they had both been tutored by Roger Ascham. They both remembered their simultaneous imprisonment in the Tower. They were both vital and tempestuous. Robert wrote that Elizabeth wanted Irish ponies because her own geldings, some of the best horses in England, didn't run fast enough.

Despite the unlikelihood of a match between the queen and one of her own subjects, people were soon saying that Lord Robert had bewitched her. Her critics complained that she was "entirely given over to love, hunting, hawking and dancing, consuming day and night with trifles. . . . He who invents most ways of wasting time is regardede as one worthy of honour." That most inventive fellow was clearly her ever-present friend, Robert Dudley, and her relationship with him was reckless and open. Dudley had frequently been with her at Hatfield and her several manor houses during the months before Mary's death.

Nicholas Hilliard, one of the few admired English painters of the time, painted this miniature portrait of Elizabeth I in 1572, when she was thirty-eight years old. NATIONAL PORTRAIT GALLERY, LONDON.

Robert Dudley, Earl of Leicester, at the age of forty-four, painted by Nicholas Hilliard in 1576. Robert was the son of John Dudley, Duke of Northumberland, whom Mary beheaded for seizing the throne in the name of Jane Grey. NATIONAL PORTRAIT GALLERY, LONDON.

Lord Robert was a handsome man, tall and dark, slim and athletic. Some people called him the Gypsy. Elizabeth sometimes called him Robin; she also named him Eyes, as she called Cecil Spirit, for Robert's eyes were beautiful, slanted, with a piercing gaze, and he was an invaluable informant who saw everything. He understood her acid wit and dished it back to her.

Dudley was so interested in theater that he sponsored his own company of actors; the flowering of Elizabethan drama that made a place for Shakespeare's talent would owe much to Robert Dudley's support and influence. He hunted and danced at Elizabeth's side, advised her in a more personal way than her much older councilors, conversed with her, and provided her with a friendship as close as a queen could have. She whose wild spirit had been governed all her life by public opinion and the tight rein of her overseers now governed them and everybody else in the realm. Elizabeth would do as she pleased.

What she pleased to do shocked everybody, but she didn't care; throughout her reign she took a perverse pleasure in being naughty enough to shock. She had denied herself pleasure during Mary's reign, confining herself to austere clothes and a simple life so as not to draw disapproval. Now she would enjoy the excitement of courtship. She encouraged the jostling of the splendid men around her as they competed for her glance, her laughter at a joke, a moment of personal conversation.

Although he quickly had become Elizabeth's favorite, Robert had many deadly enemies. To begin with, both his grandfather and his father had been executed as traitors. Robert had cleansed his reputation somewhat, but he was still a suspicious character. He had served Philip and the interests of Spain. And he was so blatantly ambitious and arrogant that other men distrusted him.

Even worse, Robert Dudley had been married for years.

Robert Dudley, Earl of Leicester, in 1575. National Portrait Gallery, London.

10
SWEET ROBIN

ROBERT DUDLEY HAD MARRIED Amy Robsart in 1551 at approximately the age of seventeen. (Communities did not always keep exact records of births, deaths, and marriages in the sixteenth century.) The couple had no children. Amy lived obscurely in the country and never came to court. Although Robert visited her rarely, his household records show that he did not neglect his wife's material needs; she spent considerable amounts of money on clothes. No provisions were made at court for the wives and children of courtiers unless they held some title of their own. Palace lodgings were so crowded that courtiers rented houses in town if they wished occasionally to see their wives. Amy was a country squire's daughter, inexperienced and perhaps hardly literate, a woman who would not have shone in the glittering splendor of the palace.

Except for these vague facts, little is known of Robert's relationship to Amy. Whatever the truth may be, people at the time whispered that the queen was in love with a married man. When one reads gossip about Elizabeth, though, either criticism or praise, it must be remembered that partisanship among her contemporaries was fierce. The Catholics hated her interference in their religious doc-trine. The Puritans hated her defense of ritual as well as her dancing and gaiety. So a Puritan might say that she spent all her time in frivolous pleasures, while her male officials complained that she dabbled too much in government details that would be better left to sensible men. It is very difficult to figure out the truth.

One of the great controversies about Elizabeth's character is the question of her sexuality. In the face of prying curiosity she cultivated the image of herself as the Virgin Queen along with the myths of Good Queen Bess and Gloriana. The propaganda was so successful that the image has stuck for four hundred years. It is a haunting idea, this vision of a great queen who had everything else but denied herself love.

Some people are uncomfortable imagining that an icon, the goddess Eliza-beth, might have felt physical desire. At least one long book has been written to defend her chastity; but without clear evidence, who can know? And how could such an emotional woman have lived without passion? Other biographers have speculated that she may have been pregnant when Katherine Parr sent her away from the temptations that Thomas Seymour offered. If so, surrounded by a large household of servants, how could the birth of a baby have been kept secret?

The curiosity about Elizabeth's virginity is in itself peculiar. Nobody writes about virgin kings; nobody writes very much at all about kings' private lives—or at least nobody did until modern times, when the royalty of England and the presidents of the United States have been subjected to the scrutiny of profes-sional busybodies. If King Philip caroused in Brussels when he was the husband of Mary Tudor, no one paid much attention. But the uproar about Elizabeth's relationship with her horse master, and her virginity, has never subsided.

This human curiosity is all the more striking because no one can know what really happened or how Elizabeth felt. She kept no journal, and few personal letters survive. The documentary evidence is sketchy. She was seen to kiss Robert at a crossroads once, on the lips as spouses do. He once took her handkerchief in a familiar way and wiped his face during a tennis match; a courtier challenged him for this public impertinence. Early one morning, Elizabeth was talking with Robert in her bedroom when he handed her an undergarment, as if he knew his way around her boudoir.

Kenilworth Castle was her gift to Dudley, and other grants of money, business licenses, and land made him enormously rich; she appointed him to the council in 1562, which gave him the political power he craved. She tickled his neck during the ceremony in 1564 that elevated him to Earl of Leicester. After Robert's death, she once removed from the drawer of a bedroom chest a miniature portrait of the beloved friend she called "Sweet Robin," carefully wrapped in paper, and showed it to a guest.

These are the particulars that biographers have interpreted again and again. But there is other tantalizing gossip in the diplomatic correspondence, reports from foreign ambassadors to their governments. These, of course, might have been red herrings, what modern governments call "disinformation," planted by the English government to mislead its enemies: official lies.

One can hardly imagine a prudent man like Cecil complaining to foreign diplomats about his queen's love affairs unless his motives were devious. Nevertheless, the Spanish ambassador who replaced Feria, Alvaro de Quadra, a notorious buyer and seller of gossip, reported that Cecil had done so. Saying that Dudley would be "better off in Paradise," Cecil allegedly begged de Quadra to advise the queen to come to her senses, for her very crown was at stake. A scandalous affair, the envoy wrote, was common knowledge among members of the privy council. Elizabeth was governed by lust, "a passionate ill-advised woman" with "a hundred thousand devils in her body," who had neither "brains nor conscience."

Gossips suffered questioning, imprisonment, and threats of execution; some had their tongues and ears cut off. Nevertheless, it was said that the queen visited Robert in his rooms day and night, and that his apartment adjoined hers. A spy in Elizabeth's household sold Spain a story that Kate Ashley had confronted Elizabeth on her knees and begged the queen to marry; the rumor that she was involved in an illicit affair with Dudley was destroying her reputation all over Europe.

According to the report, Elizabeth laughed at Kate's concern. The idea that she might be anybody's lover was ridiculous, she said, since she was never alone, but was always in the midst of hubbub. Whatever she did, everyone saw. Haughty as always, however, she went on to say that "if she ever had the will or had found pleasure in such a dishonourable life—from which God preserve her—she did not know of anyone who could forbid her." In other words, the queen herself would decide how she should behave.

What is known for certain is that Europe was abuzz with shocking talk about the Queen of England's love life, and the *appearance* of dishonor mattered more than sin. If her reputation as a virtuous woman were soiled, no royal suitor would ever marry her. The double standard was clearly operating: A king might do as he wished and nobody would stop him, but a queen must guard her reputation for purity. Elizabeth's enemies were taking full advantage of the difference.

People said that Lord Robert's country wife was ill and melancholy, suffering from a disease of the breast that was probably cancer. Rumors charged him and the queen with plotting to poison Amy, in order to free them to marry.

The only conspiracies that were revealed, however, were schemes to assassinate Elizabeth and Robert. Dudley's enemies loathed the thought of his becoming consort to the queen, effectively the king, whether crowned or not. Indeed, one of Elizabeth's own chamber servants was implicated in a plot. Cecil warned the queen to accept no gifts, no perfumed gloves or underclothes that might be tainted with poisons absorbed through the skin. No food from outside the palace kitchens was to be admitted to her quarters. The doors to her chambers were secured by armed guards.

In September 1560 Amy Dudley's servants found her lying dead at the foot of a staircase at a friend's country house, where she was staying. Her head was askew because of a broken neck, but her headdress was still neatly in place. Although he was found innocent at a hearing, thousands of gossips accused the queen's sweetheart, Robert Dudley, of arranging his wife's murder.

From this distance in time, nobody knows for sure whether Dudley was guilty. The violent death of Amy Dudley was not advantageous to him, for the scandal made marriage to the queen impossible, even if she had agreed. No expression of his grief or even regret survives, but in his correspondence, anxiously seeking information about his wife's death and damage to his own reputation, he sounds genuinely bewildered and uninformed.

A modern doctor who studied the record has noted that, in half of the people with advanced breast cancer, tumors spread to the spine. Cancer makes bones brittle and causes spontaneous fractures. Amy may have tripped on the stairs and broken her neck with the sudden movement; even the small shocks of walking down the stairs could have caused the bones in her neck to collapse.

It says a great deal about the cynicism of the period that, although Robert was never officially accused, people all over England and Europe *assumed* that he and the queen had rid themselves of the embarrassing wife so that they might marry. "The Queen of England is going to marry her horsekeeper," Mary of Scotland said contemptuously, "who has killed his wife to make room for her." Dudley was banished from court in disgrace until the scandal died down.

Perhaps Elizabeth herself never knew the truth about Amy Dudley's death. But she might have wondered about the hazards of marrying a man who had possibly disposed of his wife to advance his own interests, a fate that called up her own mother's ghost.

Ten years later, asked why she had not married Dudley, Elizabeth replied, "The aspiration to greatness and honour which is in me could not suffer him as a companion and a husband." In other words, she could not stomach marriage to her subject. To raise any Englishman to the throne would have unleashed conflict. As her favorite, Dudley remained in her control. As her husband, his status and power would have risen infinitely; others would consider him her governor, her natural superior. Perhaps Elizabeth had no intention of handing over her power to a husband of any rank. She even said so half the time—when she wasn't saying that in due time she would marry.

Whatever her motives, she kept Robert dangling, as she did archdukes, princes, and kings. But Elizabeth did reward him. With her gifts of Kenilworth Castle and other rich lands, a title, licenses to collect fees on cloth that was sold, and a place on the privy council, she raised his social and political position. Thus she established another center of influence among the councilors, a counterweight to Cecil's power.

Now Cecil and Dudley were forced to vie for Elizabeth's ear. Throughout her career she would bring forward one favorite or another, raise one man to eminence and cast another one down. In doing so she kept the power brokers off balance and unable to anticipate her next move. She also made it plain that she was no man's puppet, but was herself the power behind her throne.

Unlike modern European heads of state, Elizabeth herself financed the government, even paying military expenses, and supported the court from her own purse. Her annual income never exceeded 300,000 pounds, and that money built warships and guns, fed soldiers, paid government workers, constructed and maintained public buildings, and covered all other expenses that modern people routinely pay for with their taxes. In an emergency such as war, Parliament would agree to tax Elizabeth's subjects. She tried to avoid the people's resentment, however.

The support of Elizabeth's huge household cost 40,000 pounds a year. She had reduced the number of servants that Henry had kept. Nevertheless, household expenses rose despite her efforts, partly because of dishonesty. According to one report, she paid one year for some 20,000 sheep and lambs, 600,000 gallons of beer, and more than 4 million eggs. Hundreds of cooks and other kitchen workers were among her staff. If each occasionally sold a dozen eggs or stole a chicken for his family, the cost would amount to a huge financial loss. Elizabeth therefore looked for ways to save a penny.

Some 80 percent of the people lived in the country, and there were only about ten significant towns in England. With a population of ninety thousand, London was the largest capital in Europe. During the summer Elizabeth escaped the noise, heat, and smells of the city, as well as the epidemics that worsened in the heat of a season when food spoiled quickly and the fleas that carried the plague were active. Although nobody knew then that fleas carried the disease from rats to humans, everyone was aware that crowded cities were unhealthy in the summertime.

These trips were no small jaunts to the country with an overnight bag. A progress, as Elizabeth's visit to the areas surrounding London was called, required a caravan of 400 wagons and 2,400 pack horses. For she took the government and the royal household with her—councilors and lesser officials, private servants, laundresses and seamstresses, stablemen to groom and feed the horses, cooks and doctors, builders and drivers.

The luggage included the queen's clothes and jewels, documents, dishes, utensils, furniture and linens, equipment and tools to keep the horses and wagons going, and all the other things that her mob of companions would need on the trip. A suitably royal bed that could be dismantled and reassembled went with the queen.

On her progresses Elizabeth could observe with her own eyes the mood of her people and the state of the realm. Allowing the common people to see and even approach her, these journeys also established her reputation more deeply as Good Queen Bess. Everywhere she went, she told her subjects how she loved them and reminded them often that they loved her. She listened politely to their awkward speeches. Once she stood in the rain to watch a schoolboys' pageant. When fireworks went awry and burned down a commoner's house, Good Queen Bess had a new one built for the man.

Ordinary people received extraordinary kindness and grace from their queen. In one town the women prepared a banquet for her of 160 different foods. She ate the delicious dishes without having them tasted first, dramatically displaying her trust, and asked that some of the food be sent to her lodgings. Such an honor would have buoyed a plain woman for life.

Since even the main roads out of London were only cart tracks, unpaved dirt ruts that broke the axles of the carts and became bogs during rainstorms, the company could travel only ten or twelve miles each day. The procession raised such a cloud of dust that the provisions went on ahead. Elizabeth followed at a distance, sometimes on horseback, sometimes riding in a litter.

Everyone stayed at her courtiers' estates. The queen thereby passed on to the courtiers themselves the cost of entertaining and feeding the royal household. The result was economy—for her. Needless to say, the courtiers looked upon the honor with mixed feelings. Once a farmer approached the travelers and asked, "Which is the queen?" Elizabeth identified herself and asked what he wanted. He said that her men had seized so many of his fowl to feed her court that he was ruined. According to stories at the time, Elizabeth ordered the responsible official hanged.

Despite the cost, the aristocrats competed with each other to impress Elizabeth, for their livelihood depended on her favor. Some of them expanded their

Like her father, Elizabeth maintained great wooded estates, where she loved to hunt stags. A huntsman hands her a knife for the ceremonial slitting of a dead stag's throat. MANSELL COLLECTION.

houses or even built new ones to accommodate the court; nevertheless, many courtiers had to sleep in tents on the lawn. When they complained, Elizabeth wryly suggested that they stay home and make room for younger, more robust men who had strength and nerve to match her own.

Both Robert Dudley and William Cecil frequently hosted the queen at the estates that her generosity had enabled them to own. First one man rose in her esteem and then the other. Consequently, neither ever monopolized power in her government, as Cardinal Wolsey had done in Henry's. Now, in 1562, it was Robert Dudley, her master of the horse, who was riding high.

Influenced by him, the queen sent a military expedition into France to assist the Huguenots, the Protestant faction in the civil war there. Elizabeth for once set aside her principles against helping rebels. Mary Tudor's loss of Calais had hurt more than English pride, for the port had been a military foothold on the Continent. Still galled by its loss, Elizabeth hoped not only to weaken her enemies but also to regain the territory. She agreed to send forty thousand pounds to support the Huguenots. She also sent seven thousand soldiers against the Catholic French, commanded by Dudley's brother, a man with almost no military experience.

As the army embarked, however, Elizabeth felt ill. She took a long bath, something she and other people of her time rarely did, preferring to wash at a basin. After her daily walk in the garden of Hampton Court Palace, her illness worsened, and she went to bed with a high fever. Her servants called Dr. Burcot, a respected but bad-tempered German physician. His diagnosis was smallpox, a common and very infectious disease that had recently caused the deaths of others at court. The infection produced a rash worse than severe acne, which stung as if nettles had brushed the skin. It also caused terrible headaches, back pain, and an extremely sore throat. Sometimes it affected the victim's heart rhythm. The skin of anyone who survived smallpox was usually scarred deeply for life.

Hearing Dr. Burcot pronounce what might be a death sentence, Elizabeth was so furious she ordered her servants to throw "the knave" out. Her temperature rose, and she fell unconscious. Believing that the queen was dying, the council met to decide upon a successor. They wrangled for three days and nights. Robert Dudley assembled an army of six thousand troops around the palace. He prepared to head off any armed attack by the Scottish queen's friends or other factions that might seize upon Elizabeth's death to usurp the throne.

The queen surprised everybody by regaining consciousness, eating a little chilled meat broth, and dictating her will. Although he could not be king, she wished Robert Dudley to rule as Lord Protector of England, as Edward Seymour and John Dudley had ruled in young Edward's behalf. He was to be granted twenty thousand pounds a year so he could live in a style suitable to a ruler. Elizabeth made provisions for servants, including five hundred pounds a year (a very large sum) for the groom who slept in Dudley's bedchamber. That gift looked like a bribe to keep the servant quiet, but she declared that, as God was her witness, though she loved Dudley dearly, they had never done anything improper: They had never been lovers.

The Queen of England was preparing for death. A servant hastened to Dr. Burcot, who refused to come back because of the insult he had suffered. "By God's pestilence!" he sputtered. "Call me a knave for my good will! If she be sick, let her die!" The messenger drew a knife and threatened to kill the physician unless he came immediately to the palace and attended the queen. Burcot gave in.

At her bedside, the doctor said that he had come "almost too late." He wrapped Elizabeth's body in red cloth, leaving only her face and one hand exposed, and moved her near the fire. The cloth and the extreme heat were part of the so-called red treatment that people once thought cured smallpox. Seeing a rash appear on her bare hand, she asked what it was. "'Tis the pox," said Dr. Burcot. She began to lament. "God's pestilence!" he retorted. "Which is better? To have the pox in the hand or in the face, or in the heart and kill the whole body?"

Even after Elizabeth's gradual recovery, she remained secluded in her rooms for some time as the sores on her face healed; in the end she probably bore pockmarks for the rest of her life. Robert Dudley's sister, who had risked her own life to nurse the queen, fell ill and was so horribly scarred that she withdrew to the country and remained out of sight until she died years later.

Nobody would ever forget the thirty-year-old queen's brush with death and the crisis it had visited on a nation with no undisputed heir. Over the long term, the resulting anxiety would force Parliament and the council to step up their pressure for a royal marriage during Elizabeth's childbearing years; after that they would urge her to name a successor.

In the short term the sick queen was unable to govern the soldiers she had launched on the morning after her illness began, and the responsibility fell to Dudley. The move against France was bold, but once her troops were committed abroad, Elizabeth and her advisers lost their nerve and ordered the army to dig in rather than enter the battle. The Huguenot stronghold of Newhaven fell, and the French Protestants began to arrange a compromise with the Catholics. Calais remained in French hands. And the English troops, dying in great numbers of bubonic plague, brought the fleas that carried the disease home with them in their clothes and luggage.

This resurgence of the Black Death quickly spread throughout the country; one in five of London's population died. The superstitious English said the disease was God's vengeance for sin. Catholics and Protestants blamed each other. Elizabeth fled to Windsor Castle, where the town erected a gallows to hang travelers from London, who they feared would bring the plague with them.

Cecil seems to have watched the French fiasco from a distance, perhaps happy to see Dudley's bad judgment revealed. Unlike the earlier Scottish conflict, which

Cecil had managed, this expedition had been a disastrous loss. Elizabeth had made crucial decisions against Cecil's advice, perhaps wishing to put him in his place, but she had lost her gamble.

Once again she had trusted her fate to distant military commanders, who this time had failed her and had lost a fortune that England could not afford to waste. Reacting to her costly mistake, Elizabeth would be skittish about foreign entanglements and military actions for the rest of her reign.

Mary, Queen of Scots in 1578. Her dark, austere gown suggests mourning, and her crucifix reminds the viewer that she remained a steadfast Roman Catholic throughout her captivity.
NATIONAL PORTRAIT GALLERY, LONDON.

11
THE TROUBLESOME QUEEN OF SCOTS

Mary, Queen of Scots and Queen of France had everything she wanted except England. Since she was nearly six feet tall at a time when most women were no taller than five feet four, her presence was commanding. Her chestnut hair set off creamy skin.

Although her portraits are not particularly striking to a modern eye, the people of her time agreed that Mary was beautiful, and the French had taught her to flirt. She had a reputation for seducing any man she was determined to control. Professional courtiers, practical, cynical men sent by Elizabeth as messengers, returned without information, not only having failed in their mission to persuade Mary to change a position, but also half in love with her and befuddled by their loss of common sense. The Earl of Shrewsbury, a tough and loyal man who was trusted to guard her, was accused by his wife, Bess of Hardwick, of making love to the Queen of Scots.

If the story of Elizabeth's half-sister, Mary Tudor, is like a fairy tale about a rejected child, Mary Stuart's career resembles a soap opera. She became Queen of Scots in 1542 when, only six days after her birth, her father died in despair, having been defeated in battle by the English. While Mary of Guise governed for her daughter, Mary Stuart was brought up at the French court. In 1558, at the age of fifteen, she married Francis, the French king's son.

The subsequent two years would bring unbearable grief to Mary. Francis and she were crowned King and Queen of France in 1559 after the king died from injuries he suffered in a jousting accident. That June Mary's mother died in Scotland in the midst of negotiations with the English that transferred power to a Protestant government overseen by the Earl of Moray, Mary's bastard half-brother. She was not yet eighteen in November 1560 when her husband developed an ear infection and high fever. He died a few weeks later. His mother would rule France as regent in behalf of her next son, as Moray was doing for Mary in Scotland.

Now Mary was a queen without command of a government and a woman without a husband. Profoundly aware of her own grandeur, she was determined to marry nobody who was not her equal. Before the end of the official month of mourning for her dead husband, she was already trying to arrange a marriage to the son of King Philip II of Spain, Don Carlos. The French blocked the agreement, and the prospect of an alliance between Scotland and Spain alarmed the English. The alternative, when the negotiations failed, was equally disturbing.

England's privy council worried that when she returned to Scotland the Catholic Mary would upset Moray's Protestant government. Moray was a skilled and sensible politician like Cecil, but his illegitimate birth disqualified him for the throne. Mary's religion, sympathies, upbringing, and volatile temperament would make Scotland's alliance with France all the more dangerous.

As she prepared to assume the rule of Scotland, Mary requested safe-conduct —a guarantee of safe passage through possibly hostile lands—should her ship be forced into an English port by storms in the Channel. But she refused to sign the peace treaty that Cecil had negotiated with Scotland, and she persisted in displaying England's coat of arms as if she were its queen; her doing so was a defiant and public assertion that Elizabeth's birth was illegitimate and that the "concubine's bastard" had stolen Mary's rightful place in the succession. Elizabeth refused to grant the safe-conduct, an insulting breach of international courtesy. She changed her mind, but by the time the message arrived, the Queen of Scots had already left France.

In August 1561 Mary arrived in Scotland, where, advised by the Earl of Moray and other experienced leaders, she ruled with a steady hand. She began a correspondence with her cousin Elizabeth, and they exchanged expensive gifts, but the queens were mutually suspicious. Elizabeth's doubts were justified. As one of the terms of her marriage to Francis, Mary had secretly willed Scotland to France, should she die without children; she may have had the same plan for England. Unaware of the agreement, English courtiers assured the Scottish government that Mary was Elizabeth's favorite among the claimants to the throne.

Patience and prudence might have enabled Mary to win over her cousin, but the Queen of Scots was anything but patient and prudent. She steadfastly refused to sign the peace treaty unless Elizabeth openly recognized her as heir to the English throne. That Elizabeth would not do, remembering her own experience as "second person" in the realm. An heir would attract rebels with schemes to depose Elizabeth, and to be deposed could mean death. An announcement of her successor might bring about her assassination.

"So long as I live, I shall be Queen of England. When I am dead, they shall succeed me who have the most right," Elizabeth said. Reasonable people should not expect her "in mine own life to set my winding sheet [death shroud] before mine eyes. I know the inconstancy of the English people, how they ever mislike the present government and have their eyes fixed upon that person who is next to succeed." She went on to wryly quote a proverb: "More people adore the rising sun than the setting sun."

Mary continued looking for a husband among the princes of Europe, and Elizabeth persistently disapproved of her choices, dreading the intrusion of foreign influence on the island England shared with Scotland. To gain time, perhaps, in the endless talks that preceded a royal marriage agreement, Elizabeth proposed a bridegroom of her own liking, one she thought she could control. She would recognize Mary as heir to the English throne if the Queen of Scots would marry the Protestant Robert Dudley.

Mary refused to be manipulated. She said sweetly that, attractive though Dudley was, she couldn't deprive Elizabeth of the pleasure and solace of his company. Perhaps Elizabeth never intended to let the Dudley marriage happen but was only using him as bait. In any case, Mary continued to woo Don Carlos until he fell while chasing a servant girl down a flight of stone stairs, and suffered such severe brain damage that he could no longer marry anybody. During the same year, 1564, Elizabeth named Robert Dudley the Earl of Leicester, an elevation in status that made him more nearly Mary's social equal.

The competition between Elizabeth and Mary was evident in conversations that James Melville, the Scottish ambassador to England, reported to his government. Elizabeth tried to impress Melville, wearing a new jeweled gown in a different fashion every day. She asked him whose hair was more beautiful, hers or Mary's? Who was the better dancer? Who was fairer?

The diplomat answered diplomatically: Elizabeth was the fairest queen in England, and Mary the fairest in Scotland. Then what about their comparative height? Elizabeth surely already knew Mary's precise dimensions and was goading Melville. When he said that Mary was taller, Elizabeth replied that the Queen of Scots must be too tall, since she herself was neither too tall nor too short.

Hearing that Mary hunted in her leisure time, read scholarly books, and played the lute and virginals, Elizabeth arranged a demonstration of her own musical gifts. A courtier brought Melville to a chamber where Elizabeth was playing music alone. She pretended surprise when she noticed him listening quietly. She never played for an audience, she said, but Melville thought that the whole scene was staged.

During one conversation Elizabeth declared as she often did that she preferred to live and die a virgin, unless Mary chose a husband badly and forced marriage upon her in order to protect her throne. Melville scoffed. "Madam, you need not tell me that," he said. "I know your stately stomach [pride]. You think, if you were married, you would be but Queen of England; and now you are King and Queen both. You may not endure a commander." Melville was a perceptive observer of Elizabeth's psychology.

In February 1565 Elizabeth sent another candidate for marriage to Mary: Henry Stuart, Lord Darnley, a tall, "lady-faced" nineteen-year-old boy. Like Mary, he was a grandchild of Henry VIII's sister Margaret; his grandfather was not the Scottish king, however, but Margaret's second husband, an earl. Thus both Mary and Darnley were direct descendants of Elizabeth's grandfather, King Henry VII; if they married, they would join their royal claim of Tudor blood and enhance their separate rights to the throne.

Cecil advised against sending the Catholic Darnley to Scotland; he feared the uniting of the two claims, but his counsel was overridden. Elizabeth judged that Darnley's Tudor lineage would be a sufficient lure for the Queen of Scots, but that she herself would be able to control events. The exact thinking behind Elizabeth's marriage ploys against Mary is unclear now. The strategy was generally to keep the Queen of Scots occupied with English suitors. Managed behind the scenes by Elizabeth, these flirtations delayed a match with any man who might be hostile to her interests. And Mary's desire for the English throne made her fall for the bait.

There followed a devious chess game. Elizabeth's mistake, the assumption that

Darnley would be her pawn, emerged slowly. Mary, who realized the purpose of his mission, ignored him. Elizabeth announced that she would not recognize Mary as heir even if she changed her mind and married Robert Dudley, the Earl of Leicester. Mary wept, saying that the English queen had played her for a fool, dangling Leicester, then snatching him away. In the meantime Darnley caught the measles, and Mary nursed him through the illness. By the time he recovered, the two had become involved in a love affair.

Elizabeth had disastrously misjudged the tall lad, a rare lapse of her legendary perceptiveness. When she commanded him and his father to return to London, they ignored the summons. In July 1565 Mary married Henry Stuart, Lord Darnley. Now Mary and Darnley's dual claim to the English throne was more persuasive.

Darnley soon proved himself to be a poor choice for either husband or king. He was an arrogant, willful drunkard. During a visit at an Edinburgh merchant's house, when Mary begged him to stop drinking, he spoke to her so viciously that she left the house weeping. She increasingly turned for companionship to her Italian secretary, David Riccio. Mary was pregnant, and Darnley believed that the child was the secretary's. While Mary and Riccio were eating supper, Darnley and several others burst into her apartment, dragged Riccio from the table, and before Mary's eyes stabbed him fifty-six times.

In June 1566 the Scottish ambassador Melville returned to the English court again and found Elizabeth dancing when he arrived. He whispered something to her. She sat down in dejection and held her head in her hands. "The Queen of Scots is lighter of a fair son," she said, "and I am but a barren stock." This remark is a rare suggestion of the mighty Elizabeth's sense of loss and loneliness. One pities Gloriana.

Mary had given birth to a boy, James. However, the infant had hardly been christened in the jeweled, gold baptismal basin Elizabeth sent as a gift when further shocking news arrived. If the rumors in Scotland were true, Darnley was plotting against Mary. She in turn had fallen in love with the married James Hepburn, Earl of Bothwell, another rogue, who was her lord high admiral.

Darnley fell ill, perhaps with smallpox or a sexually transmitted disease. What had seemed like the measles, when Mary and Darnley first became infatuated, may have been the first rash of syphilis. In February 1567, as he began to recover, Mary took him to an isolated house at Kirk o' Field, in Edinburgh, and stayed there with him overnight. The following night she left hurriedly, to attend a courtier's wedding party. Soon afterward an explosion blew up the house, rocking the neighborhood. Darnley's strangled body was found under a pear tree on the opposite side of the town wall that abutted the rear of the demolished building. He was still only a youth of twenty, three years younger than his widow.

Subsequent events suggest that Mary had tolerated the murder of her husband, even if she had not been actively involved. She showed no grief about Darnley's death. A week after it occurred, in fact, she stopped pretending to mourn and attended a party where Bothwell was also a guest. She gave her husband's beautiful clothing to the earl, who was under suspicion for the king's murder. At the make-believe trial Darnley's father did not present evidence he possessed, knowing that Bothwell had Mary's protection. An intimidated jury acquitted the earl.

As if events had not been melodramatic enough already, Bothwell then abducted Mary and, according to his own story, raped her. After his hurriedly arranged divorce, the Queen of Scots married her kidnapper. Europe was scandalized, more by the Catholic Mary's marriage to a divorced man than by the murder of her husband. The pope denounced her. Mobs cried out, "Burn the whore!" Posters appeared in the streets of Edinburgh bearing pictures of Mary as a lewd mermaid with a naked torso; *mermaid* was a slang word for *prostitute*. The Scottish people rose up in rebellion and imprisoned Mary at Lochleven, an island castle. She was forced to give up Bothwell, who escaped to Denmark, where he died in prison, insane. At the time of her capture Mary was pregnant, but she soon miscarried. The dead babies were twins.

Elizabeth's wisdom in refusing to name the wild Queen of Scots her successor was now more than clear. Cecil and the other councilors tried to persuade Elizabeth to rejoice at the removal of a threat to her life. Nevertheless, despite her disgust about Mary's behavior, Elizabeth's delicate feelings for royal privilege rose to the surface again. Privately she raged and ranted and threatened war to restore Mary. More controlled in public, she sent a restrained message to the rebels. Much as she abhorred the murder of her cousin, their king, and Mary's marriage to Bothwell, she wrote, "It is not lawful nor tolerable for them, being by God's ordinance subjects, to call her, who also by God's ordinance is their superior and Prince, to answer to their accusations by way of force. . . . We do not think it consonant in nature that the head should be subject to the foot." Nevertheless, holding that a queen was no more privileged to commit murder and adultery than anybody else, Mary's earls forced her to abdicate her throne. Her year-old baby was crowned King James VI.

In May 1568 Mary escaped from Lochleven and raised an army. When its action against the Scottish earls failed, she cut off her hair, disguised herself, and fled into England, expecting Elizabeth to receive her at court and help her regain her rights. Now Elizabeth faced a dilemma. Her councilors favored eliminating Mary's threat by turning her over to the Scottish government; she had, after all, schemed for years to usurp the English throne. Elizabeth refused. Although Mary's actions were appalling, she was nevertheless a queen, as Elizabeth was, and the weakening of royalty anywhere undermined the Queen of England's power.

Therefore Elizabeth bitterly refused to return Mary to her Scottish captors, though every other option was dangerous. To restore Mary to the throne would necessitate war against Protestant Scotland, which might draw France in. If she were released and sent to France, she might find support there to invade Scotland. To imprison her in England would infuriate English Catholics and enrage France, whose king was the brother of her first husband.

Finally, to allow Mary freedom in England, to grant her the respect due a queen, would implicitly sanction her claim to Elizabeth's throne. Having been identified as heir, Mary would be a political focus for everyone who yearned to bring down Elizabeth. With misgivings, doubtless remembering the pain of her own captivity in the Tower and at Woodstock, the Queen of England confined the Queen of Scots in the distant north.

Mary had escaped from Lochleven with only the clothes on her back. The Earl of Moray had already begun to sell her pearls to Elizabeth at a cut rate. All pearls came from wild oysters then and were so rare that only the wealthiest people could afford them. Elizabeth loved to wrap herself in ropes of pearls, some white, others black.

Saying that she had nothing but a borrowed red petticoat that came only to her knees, Mary asked Elizabeth to send her clothing more appropriate to her rank. A waiting woman packed a box. Mary received it in silence; according to legend, it contained only two poor undergarments, a length of black velvet, and a pair of shoes.

In 1567, during the period of Darnley's death and Mary's loss of her throne, the Spanish had sent thirty-five thousand troops to the Netherlands, enforcing King Philip II's rule on an unwilling people. Thus a hostile army stood across the Channel at England's doorstep, closer to London than Scotland was. Meanwhile, religious unrest persisted in Scotland, and religious civil war continued to boil in France.

Responsibility for leadership in the face of these dangers had worn down the thirty-four-year-old Elizabeth. Some said she was becoming so thin and physically weak that her physicians expected her not to live much longer. She was frequently ill with colds and sore throats, and she limped on an ulcerated leg when she thought she was not being watched. While everywhere the threats to England mounted, the country's sickly queen stubbornly remained an unmarried woman.

The question was not only the undecided succession. No matter what she did, short of marriage to a man who would tame her and short of childbirth, Elizabeth could not overcome the imagined inadequacy of her gender. For some of the men who were forced "unnaturally" to obey a woman, no triumph of Elizabeth's, no brilliant acts of leadership, no display of intelligence or wisdom, could unsettle their certainty that any woman was inherently and permanently incapable. These men were as affronted by the governance of a woman, their natural inferior, as Elizabeth was by the rebellion of the Scottish people against their queen. In addition, this faction wanted the safety of a secure succession.

The Earl of Leicester joined a plot against his friend and benefactor, Elizabeth, hoping to assure such an outcome. Along with the recently widowed Duke of Norfolk, Leicester and several others took matters into their own "superior" hands. They conspired to engineer a marriage between Mary, Queen of Scots, and Norfolk, on the condition that Mary support the Protestant church in Scotland. The dukedoms of John Dudley and Edward Seymour had been dissolved upon their conviction for treason. Now the only duke and therefore the greatest nobleman in England, Norfolk behaved like a king on his own estates. Wherever he went, five hundred horsemen accompanied him. He was related to three queens—Anne Boleyn, Katherine Howard, and Elizabeth herself—and now he planned to marry another. Leicester and the other plotters thought that, with an Englishman as Scottish king, Mary would cease to be a threat. More important, her marriage to Norfolk would legitimize her claim to the English throne.

Like many another clumsy plot of the time, this one miscalculated the feeling of the Scottish people, who would not have had Mary back. Cecil's spies quickly

Elizabeth's closely ranked soldiers, wearing armor, on the march. BODLEIAN LIBRARY.

discovered the treason and informed Elizabeth. When Norfolk defied her summons, she fainted in a rage, and her servants revived her with sniffs of vinegar. Norfolk was sent to the Tower, and the conspiracy collapsed. Realizing that his disloyalty was about to be discovered, Robert Dudley took to his bed with a well-timed illness, which brought an anxious Elizabeth to his side. He confessed everything; as he had trusted, she forgave it all.

A combination of factors triggered further trouble. Norfolk had allied himself with the earls of the northern border regions of England, Westmorland and Northumberland. That alignment, associated with the Catholic convictions of the countryside, the loyalty of the people to their local leaders, and sympathy for Mary, in 1569 resulted in another uprising. The northern earls hoped to liberate Mary and restore Catholicism. Their rebellion was both a political revolution and a religious crusade, for the earls felt that their duty to the pope was a higher calling than loyalty to the queen. They began their campaign with a Mass at Durham Cathedral, and their procession of soldiers was led by priests. The army carried religious banners and other symbols into battle.

Queen Elizabeth's troops put down the rebellion with minimal killing, but the aftermath was bloody. Gentlemen escaped or bought their freedom, but the common people suffered. Soldiers burned the crops and destroyed stored food. The animals on which the people's lives depended were led away to feed the army or to be shipped south. Since loyal subjects could not be identified, Cecil suggested that villagers be tortured or starved until they named the guilty. Hoping to discourage future rebellions, soldiers killed hundreds of farmers and other workers. They executed random groups of townspeople in the numbers they estimated had joined the uprising. The army hanged eighty people in the town of Durham alone.

While she may not have issued the orders directly, Elizabeth was aware of everything that happened in her kingdom. Good Queen Bess must have known that corpses littered northern England.

12
A VERY PUBLIC PRIVATE LIFE

EVEN IN THE MIDST OF REVOLUTION and strife, queens and presidents, like everybody else, are human beings with personal lives and spotty characters. People don't like to suppose that great leaders are creatures of human proportions who occasionally develop toothaches, tell lies, give in to temper, and otherwise behave badly, as all humans do. Such faults suggest that leaders may fail in leadership, too. Elizabeth's failings raised a constant undercurrent of disapproval, and her personality influenced her policies. Like other strong characters, she developed an emphatic personal style.

She was "not a morning woman," she said, arising at eight o'clock in the morning, much later than her fifteen hundred servants. She liked to wake up with a fast walk alone around the formal gardens that surrounded her palaces. At Richmond she had ten acres of orchards and gardens where her workmen grew not only flowers but fruits and vegetables, greens, and herbs for use in the palace's eight kitchens. Some live plants were brought to her from the New World; by mid-century, potatoes and tobacco had arrived in Europe. Six hundred cherry trees were ordered at once for the orchard at Hampton Court Palace. If the weather was stormy, Elizabeth walked in the gallery, but she preferred to be outdoors.

The girl whose contemporaries had criticized her for Puritanical simplicity during Mary Tudor's reign had changed her taste. She spent seven hundred pounds on clothes in one year, as much as a nobleman's annual income, and she received many more garments as gifts. One annual inventory listed "67 rounde gowns, 100 loose gowns, 102 French gowns, 99 robes, 127 cloaks, 56 outer skirts, and 18 lappe mantles," among other things.

The clothes the queen wore in public were so ornate that she needed the help of her ladies to dress in eight layers, including smock, bodice, petticoat, hoops, skirt, kirtle, gown, and sleeves, each with laces and fasteners to keep it in place. The separate sleeves were pinned or tied to the lowcut bodice that revealed her white bosom. The bodice was mounted on a rigid wooden framework that came to a point several inches below the natural waist, a fashion that created the illusion of a long torso and a tiny waist. It must have been drudgery for the queen merely to get dressed and hard labor to carry around her heavy gold and fur-trimmed velvet. But she had to wear the costume to play the role of Gloriana.

She dressed more simply in her private quarters, with only her close friends about her. There she set aside the Gloriana image, removed her wig, and wore a loose gown, which was something like a modern housecoat. But for public appearances her ladies curled and dressed Elizabeth's thinning hair and filled it out with rolls and curls and hanks; as she grew older and more gray, she wore increasingly extravagant red wigs. Lace ruffs rose from her neck like fanciful haloes. At her waist hung a pomander, a perfumed container that she sniffed when she was overpowered by the odors of people who rarely sat down in a bath-tub. She liked the smell of marjoram.

Some of her huge colored jewels imitated animals, birds, or flowers. After someone gave her knitted silk stockings as a gift, she always wore them, a new pair every week, though they scandalized the righteous: They revealed the shape of her leg when she flounced her floor-length skirt. To stay warm in her drafty palaces, which were heated only by fireplaces even in the dead of winter, she wore fur cloaks and muffs.

Like other women of her time, Elizabeth used heavy cosmetics made of borax, alum, powdered eggshell, and oil. The white cream that smoothed her pockmarks contrasted harshly with the red rouge on her cheeks and lips. To imitate her naturally pale skin, her contemporaries spread whiteners on their faces and colored their lips bright red. They were unaware that the ingredients of some of these makeups, notably lead and mercury, were poisons that blackened the teeth, coarsened the skin, and destroyed the brain.

Men as well as women painted their faces. The courtiers also dyed their trimmed beards bright colors such as orange and purple with gold specks, to match their brilliant clothes. Some courtiers spent so much on their wardrobes that it was said they wore their fortunes on their backs. Their success depended on their attracting the attention of the queen amid the color and noise and hullabaloo of the court.

Elizabeth usually ate alone in her privy chamber, her private sitting room, where she picked at her food and had little appetite for anything but sweets. Her meals were light, with fish and fowl more often than red meat. The ale called "angel's face" or "dragon's milk" that most people drank regularly was too strong for her; she diluted her wine and beer with water. Her main meal was served at noon; she ate supper at five; and a Good Night ceremony at nine o'clock in the evening brought ale and white bread, not the coarse bread made of rye or dry ground peas that common people ate. The food was served on silver and gold. Elizabeth and her courtiers used knives and spoons and jeweled gold toothpicks, but forks, recently invented in Italy, had not yet been brought to England.

Elizabeth's personal attendants were on call twenty-four hours a day; someone was always with her. Servants bustled everywhere, laying the fires, rubbing the wood paneling in the palaces till it shone. According to a modern plaque at Tintern Abbey, the brass they polished was a new invention, an alloy mixed in precise proportions at exact temperatures. The window glass, another new fashion, was also a great luxury.

The high-spirited young ladies of the court mocked their patron in private among themselves, ridiculing her exaggerated femininity and manner. The Countess of Shrewsbury, Bess of Hardwick, one of Mary Stuart's Catholic partisans, wrote that she and the Countess of Lennox—Darnley's mother and Elizabeth's cousin—could hardly restrain their snickering when they talked with the queen.

Her male courtiers also disparaged Elizabeth. "They labour under two things at this Court," said one observer, "delay and inconstancy, which proceeded from the sex of the queen." "This fiddling woman troubles me out of measure," said another. "God's wounds! This it is to serve a base, bastard, pissing kitchen woman! If I had served any prince in Christendom, I had not been so dealt withal."

At the same time that they demeaned actual women's practical ability, Elizabeth's courtiers adored the ideal of noble womanhood. Thus courtiers might complain because of her gender one moment and flatter her the next, unable to adjust to being ruled by a woman. While they cursed her behind her back, to her face the men around Elizabeth made a sophisticated game of compliments, according to the tradition of courtly love that had influenced manners and the arts since the Middle Ages. She was said to equal the Greek and Roman goddesses, with virtue like the chaste Diana's, the wisdom of Athena, and the beauty of Venus. Her courtiers outdid each other writing witty riddles and verse to praise the queen. They told her that nobody dared look at her face, for it shone as brightly as the sun.

According to a charming legend, Sir Walter Raleigh once spread his costly new cloak in a puddle to protect the queen's feet from the mud. In such words

Sir Walter Raleigh and his son in 1602, the year before Elizabeth's death. Elizabethan aristocrats dressed their children as miniature adults. The boy even wears a sword and imitates his father's stance. NATIONAL PORTRAIT GALLERY, LONDON.

and actions there was a great deal of ironic humor; the witty queen and her courtiers alike were amused by the outlandish flattery. And yet Elizabeth was vain; everybody knew that when she played cards or chess she expected to win, and compliments from her ladies were required.

In addition to this playacting, a people who had lost the beautiful imagery and traditions of the old religion translated their devotion to the Virgin Mary into love of Queen Elizabeth. Such customs and attitudes are evident not only in the written record but in artists' portraits as well. In different paintings Elizabeth stands on a map of England, rests her hand on a globe, or holds the rainbow in her hand. Her gowns are embroidered with eyes and ears, suggesting her knowledge of all things, or with a serpent, a symbol of wisdom. She appears with an ermine on her arm or a sieve in her hand, both symbols associated with chastity.

Other more practical concerns influenced Elizabeth's portraits as well, for the government used them as a propaganda tool. No image of her could be printed without a license. And of course the government refused to license the Elizabethan equivalent of modern political cartoons, such as a French drawing of Elizabeth on horseback, dressed in finery but lewdly hitching up her dress to display her backside. Although officials were not able to eliminate such scathing pictures entirely, surviving portraits idealize the queen. Paintings composed in Elizabeth's old age present her as a fair young goddess. There was a brisk market for such art. Courtiers wore miniature pictures of her as ornaments, and gentlemen wanted portraits to hang on their walls; thousands of poorer people bought metal medallions or prints.

Everybody who saw her noticed the beauty of her long-fingered hands, which she contrived to display. Other traits are uncertain, however. According to different documents her skin was either white or ruddy or swarthy, her eyes were either gray or brown or green, and she was either tall or short, depending on who described her. One witness said that she became fat as she aged, another that she was emaciated.

Elizabeth was nervous and suffered frequent toothaches and abscesses. For dental care people used a linen cloth and powdered brick, coral, or pumice, harsh abrasives that wore off tooth enamel. The Bishop of London allowed one of his own good teeth to be pulled, to prove to her that the pain could be withstood, before Elizabeth would permit the removal of her own bad tooth; without anesthetics, people felt the full brunt of the pain. Late in her life ambassadors reported that one side of Elizabeth's face was sunken, because she had lost so many teeth and did not have the modern benefit of well-fitted false ones. Some of the teeth that remained in her mouth were, like those of most English people at the time, black with decay.

Queen Elizabeth talked in a loud voice, and her palace echoed with her hearty laughter. When she was not speaking honeyed words, she used earthy language, outswearing the men around her. Her oaths, according to a writer of the time, included "by God and by Christ, and by many parts of his glorified body, and by saints, faith, troth and other things." One courtier had the misfortune to pass gas noisily when he bowed to her. He was so embarrassed that he left the court for seven years. When he returned, the queen greeted him by saying, "My Lord, I had forgot the Fart."

Nevertheless, she could be charming when she wished. Sir John Harington, one of some hundred godsons, viewed her with a mixture of affection and fear: "When she smiled, it was a pure sunshine that everyone did choose to bask in if they could; but anon came a storm from a sudden gathering of clouds, and the thunder fell in wondrous manner on all alike." (It was Harington who invented the flushing toilet and installed one in the palace for Elizabeth.) Her lord chancellor said of her, "The Queen did fish for men's souls, and she had so sweet a bait that no one could escape her network."

Still, she was notorious for her temper; unlike ordinary people's anger, her tantrums were recorded. Although she was fond of her maids of honor, she struck one so hard, according to the gossips, that she broke the lady's finger. She stabbed another's hand with a knife for serving food clumsily. She shouted at her officials and slapped them in public. Her councilors suffered such abuse as the frequent threat to make them "shorter by a head." Francis Walsingham, called Elizabeth's Moor because of his dark skin and eyes, followed William Cecil as secretary of state and object of abuse; once he ducked the queen's hurled slipper. Overpowered by fury, she sometimes withdrew and read or translated Greek and Latin into English until she had composed herself. Reading was more than a sedative, however. She studied every day throughout her life.

Elizabeth spent her afternoons receiving ambassadors in the presence chamber, among her own courtiers and politicians. Despite the weight of her ornate clothing, she stood throughout these long interviews, even in old age. People admired Elizabeth's intelligence and learning. Diplomats marveled about her grasp of European politics and history. Her knowledge of languages enabled her to converse with foreign ambassadors in their own tongues or unexpectedly to deliver a brilliant speech in Latin, the international language, as if it were easy. She said that she was more afraid of making a mistake in her Latin than she was of death.

Sometimes officials came late at night with papers, and she often worked when she couldn't sleep. But evening was also a time for pleasure and relaxation. She enjoyed playing cards and chess, and she kept small pets about, including dogs, birds, and apes. Decent ordinary people in Elizabeth's time were in their houses at sundown, sheltered from the thieves who roamed the unlit streets. Workers were asleep by nine o'clock, since they began their labors before dawn broke. The court, however, stayed up late for entertainment.

Loving music as her father had, the queen maintained a choir of fifty singers, and more than forty instrumentalists. Musicians whose compositions are still famous, such as William Byrd and Thomas Tallis, were her employees. (The fact that Byrd was a Catholic reflected the queen's liberality.) She sang well, in addition to her skill in playing the lute, lyre, and virginals.

The first printing press had been introduced in England shortly after its invention late in the fifteenth century. People bought books in increasing numbers, especially books about wonders in the New World. Theatrical companies,

Londoners flocked to the Globe Theater, which thrived despite religious opposition from the Puritans. A replica of the Globe opened in 1997. FOLGER SHAKE-SPEARE LIBRARY.

including William Shakespeare's, performed for Queen Elizabeth. Indeed, some of his plays were written to be performed at court. The commercial theater, a new cultural invention, helped fill the emptiness many people felt during the decline of ritual and pomp in the churches.

When the queen was nearly seventy years of age, she still joined in the athletic dances of the time and critiqued the performance of her courtiers; it could almost be said that dancing was among a courtier's job requirements. The dances were so physically demanding that sometimes people broke their legs and occasionally, it was said, their necks. Men often complained that Elizabeth's endurance for standing, dancing, or riding wore them out. Through discipline and an iron will, she had trained herself to outlast the men who thought her weak, thus countering their prejudice in action.

The energetic exercises Queen Elizabeth loved included horseback riding and hunting with falcons. At fifteen she had slit the throat of a stag with her own hand. Even in her sixties, she still rode horseback ten miles at a time and hunted every other day.

And whether on progress at her courtiers' estates or at a London palace, she enjoyed bearbaiting, a fight staged between a chained bear and three mastiff dogs. Although the lower classes were forbidden by law to bowl or play tennis, they were permitted to watch the torture of animals.

It seems odd that the sophisticated Elizabethan court should have enjoyed such vulgar cruelty. But even Shakespeare's great plays, for all their gorgeous

Elizabethans went to the Bear Garden as modern people go to the football stadium, for entertainment. Trainers goaded dogs and chained bears to fight until they tore each other apart. BY PERMISSION OF THE BRITISH LIBRARY.

language and noble thoughts, feature low characters whose comedy brings pretensions down to scale. In fact the dramas of Shakespeare, who was born in 1564 and became the greatest playwright of Elizabeth's reign, were performed before standing audiences at the Globe Theater. The Globe was located near the Thames, nearby an arena for bearbaiting. A witness of one such display reported "such expens of blood az a months licking [would] not recover." In the Elizabethans' view, the bloodier the better. People were accustomed to seeing human heads mounted at the gates of towns.

The presence of the Globe and the bear pit on the same riverbank is a fitting example of the sixteenth century's temperament: an unnerving mix of physical vulgarity and cultural elegance. The English exaggerated these threads in the human sensibility, and they were intertwined in Elizabeth's character and knotted around her heart.

13
TO KILL THE QUEEN

ORN INTO MORTAL DANGER, Elizabeth lived her entire life with the threat of murder hanging over her head like an axe. She survived so many crises that a contemporary observed, "God must be English." Her habitual "indecisiveness" and sudden alterations of travel routes and other plans were taken as proof of her feminine weakness. Once when she had changed her mind three times about leaving Windsor Castle, she heard a workman in the courtyard below complain, "Now, I see the Queen is a woman, as well as my wife!" She laughed and threw down a coin to him. She changed the route of her travels hour by hour, whether she was going to the country or choosing a bridge across the River Thames. Her doing so, despite her servants' impatience, made it more difficult for assassins to plan an ambush.

The queen was less safe, of course, when she left the protection of her London palace and went out in public. During a ride in her barge on the Thames one day, Elizabeth and her companions heard a gunshot. A few feet away one of her men had been hit in both arms by a bullet shot from a nearby boat.

"Be of good cheer," the queen said, as she tossed her neck scarf for the man to use as a bandage. He would be well attended, she assured him.

That shot, it turned out, had been fired accidentally, as an arrow had once barely missed her during a hunt. Genuine plots against her life, however, were frequently uncovered by her government's spies. And when the pope excommunicated her at last in 1570, the danger, as she had expected, increased. Elizabeth's fear was evident in her actions. Early in her reign, hearing that an Italian poisoner had found employment in her household, she dismissed every Italian who served her. Reacting to another rumor, she seized all the keys to her privy chamber.

The queen was not safe even from her own inner circle, the noblemen at her side. The Duke of Norfolk, for example, had not given up plotting with Mary Stuart. In 1571 the Florentine banker Roberto Ridolfi obtained a promise of papal support for a Spanish invasion of England. Ridolfi had previously been involved in the 1568 scheme to arrange a marriage between Norfolk and Mary. Now Norfolk agreed to lead a rebellion to join the invasion if the Spanish would send ten thousand troops. So much for the fantasy of a queen's pampering by her adoring subjects.

The plot was fanciful; no Spanish troops came near sailing against England at that time. But nothing incensed the English more than the thought of foreign intrusion. By now the aging William Cecil had become treasurer, and Francis Walsingham had succeeded him as secretary of state, Elizabeth's top official. Walsingham's spy service discovered the plot, and the Duke of Norfolk was tried and condemned to beheading, brought down by his royal ambitions.

Though he denied involvement, King Philip II had been implicated in the Ridolfi plot. Further cause for rising tensions with Spain was its claim to ownership of the Americas. The voyage of Christopher Columbus had been financed by Catherine of Aragon's parents, Philip's great-grandparents. The pope had divided the new American territories between Spain and Portugal, shutting the treasure trove to England and France. Now a river of silver and gold flowed from "the Indies" to Philip's pocket, supporting his ambitions to conquer Europe and expand his empire to Africa.

Elizabeth tolerated and even sponsored privateers—officially privileged pirates—who attacked shipping from Spanish America. England had sent explorers in a fruitless search for the Northeast and Northwest Passages around Europe and America that Renaissance people believed existed. Soon Sir Walter Raleigh and other investors would finance the English colony on Roanoke Island, off the coast of what is now North Carolina. Sir John Hawkins would join the slave trade that had been firmly established by other nations for fifty years. By mid-century, potatoes, turkey, and chocolate, all New World foods, had been brought to Europe; people who could afford expensive imports were becoming addicted to tobacco. The rise of middle-class traders would require more and larger ships. For now, however, without significant trade or territories in the New World, England had no need for a huge oceangoing fleet such as the one Spain had built.

In 1577 the English adventurer and privateer Francis Drake, who had sailed on a slave ship with Hawkins, set sail for a voyage around the world, quietly backed by Elizabeth. The difficulty, daring, and renown of the feat made it comparable to a modern space flight. Drake returned successfully in 1580, with booty of one hundred tons of silver and one hundred pounds of gold, seized from the Spaniards. Elizabeth, who received a share of the profits, knighted him.

Drake's theft of Spanish treasure was a further cause of antagonism between Spain and England. Conflict simmered on in the Netherlands and Ireland, both places that could provide a base for an invasion of England. Hostility with Spain intensified Elizabeth's danger, personified by Mary, Queen of Scots. Parliament pressured Elizabeth to execute her cousin queen. Elizabeth refused.

Her obstinacy frustrated her worried courtiers. Since no mechanism except the order of succession existed for the nonviolent transfer of power, a deposed queen could never merely retire to private life. She and her loyalists would have to be killed to eliminate her threat to the new regime. If Elizabeth were deposed, her courtiers would die with her. Just such fear had nearly brought Elizabeth's sister to execute her at the age of twenty.

In addition to Elizabeth's reluctance to interfere with another monarch, emotional factors protected Mary Stuart. Elizabeth never forgot her misery in the Tower, while her sister contemplated her execution. Certainly she remembered her beheaded mother as well. Now she could not shed Tudor blood herself.

Mary therefore remained guarded, under arrest in the bedrooms of great houses, moving from place to place so often that her remedy for motion sickness became known. According to legend, she ate oranges cooked in sugar to settle her queasy stomach. Her French-speaking ladies called the dish "Marie's *malade*"; the English named it "marmalade." Some people claim now that they occasionally smell the scent of oranges in the room Mary once occupied at Lyme Hall, near Manchester.

Despite her danger, despite her knowledge of the pressure from Parliament to behead her, Mary would not leave well enough alone. She bided her time, working fine needlepoint patterns specially designed by artists for her pillows and chair seats. And she schemed.

Everywhere she looked, Elizabeth saw factions opposed to her rule, and Norfolk had proven that she could not trust her courtiers. Even Robert Dudley, the Earl of Leicester and Elizabeth's beloved friend, looked cautiously to the future, maintaining friendly relations with the imprisoned Mary in case she should inherit the throne after all. The French wanted a monarch sympathetic to French interests, while the Spanish wanted a friend to Spain. Elizabeth worried and wept about her danger.

Religion, of course, was inseparable from all other sources of plots against her reign. The pope's excommunication of Elizabeth had surprised no one, but that act had exposed her to growing risk, removing the duty of subjects to obey her as God's representative. Suddenly the burden of Catholics was not obedience but rebellion; they would be excommunicated by the Church if they acted as her subjects and punished by the queen if they did not.

The Catholic owners of great houses illegally smuggled missionaries into England and hid them in "priest's holes," cupboards behind panels or under floorboards. (A shriveled body was later found under the floor of Mary's room at Lyme Hall.) Radical Protestant Puritans, who said that the Book of Common Prayer had been plucked from a "popish dunghill," agitated against the regime. The government took this undercurrent of religious disobedience as treason. Between 1581 and 1588 at least eighty-four people were executed for religious reasons.

Two individuals represent Elizabeth's radical opponents and her government's harsh response. Edmund Campion, a Catholic missionary convicted of treason, swore that his duty specifically forbade involvement in politics. He had been tortured, his nails pulled from his fingers; yet as he waited to be hacked to pieces, he publicly blessed Elizabeth. A radical Protestant, John Stubbs, suffered for writing a pamphlet opposing her; as his right hand was chopped off with a cleaver struck by a mallet, he raised his hat with his left, crying, "God save the Queen," and fainted.

Stubbs's pamphlet had attacked Elizabeth's proposed marriage to Francis, Duke of Alençon, youngest brother of the French King Henry III (who had succeeded his brothers, Francis II and Charles IX). A few English councilors encouraged the match, wishing to further Alençon's military plans against the Spanish. The court still hoped for an heir, despite the physical danger that a first pregnancy would pose to a woman forty-five years old. But most Protestants, like Stubbs the pamphleteer, opposed the marriage, negotiations for which dragged on for years. They feared Alençon's Catholicism and French domination, remembering all too well the effect upon them of Mary Tudor's marriage to Philip.

Alençon had been reared in the corrupt French court, where the licentious and eccentric King Henry had now taken to wearing a basket of little dogs on a ribbon around his neck, or attending dances with the men of his court all dressed as women. Elizabeth's prospective bridegroom himself was an unattractive man more than twenty years younger than she. Smallpox had scarred his face, deeply pitting his nose, which was so large as to be deemed a deformity. His height was under five feet, though ironically one of his names was "Hercules."

Alençon's foreignness was his most obvious liability. Yet he demanded that England provide France with a port, defended by three thousand French soldiers. He intended to worship at private Catholic Masses. He would be crowned and referred to with his wife as the King and Queen of England; the order of titles, the king preceding the queen, was significant. And he sought a huge loan to finance his army's expedition against the Spanish in the Netherlands.

It is hard to believe that Elizabeth ever considered marrying such a man. Nevertheless, she carried on a flirtation, calling him her Frog. One staged scene between the supposed lovers occurred in the gallery, a crowded public room, where Elizabeth told the French ambassador in a loud voice that she intended to marry Alençon. She kissed the duke on the lips and placed a ring from her own finger on his. This act, amounting to a public and binding betrothal, astounded the court. The following morning she announced that, after a restless night, she had changed her mind. She must put the interests of her country before her own happiness, she said.

The duke left England ruefully, but with ten thousand pounds in his pocket, a gift from Elizabeth. Having seen him off, her ladies whispered, she gleefully danced in her rooms and then wrote a "lamentation" for her amusement.

Elizabeth's fling with Alençon was a theatrical ploy for her own personal and political purposes. She had learned that in 1578 her beloved Leicester, wanting

a legitimate heir, had secretly married Lettice Knollys, whom the jealous Elizabeth called the "she-wolf." The queen was so hurt that she briefly imprisoned
Leicester. Her dalliance with Alençon punished Leicester for his deception. It
also used France against Spain.

Disorder persisted on the Continent. Religious massacres had exploded in
France. Prince William of Orange, the uncrowned Protestant leader of the
northern Netherlands, was assassinated in his own house after Philip offered a
reward for the murder of this "enemy of the human race." Extremists on both
sides preached sedition as a holy act.

In the 1580s agents conducted house-to-house searches in London and
locked up political suspects, priests, and strangers. Executions increased. Soon
after the death of William of Orange in 1584, Dr. William Parry, a former spy
in Walsingham's service and member of the House of Commons, was arrested
for plotting to kill the queen.

The spy had bragged publicly that he and an accomplice would ride alongside
the queen's carriage on horseback, one man on each side, and shoot her in the head
with a bullet blessed by the pope. According to another story, Parry had once passed
Elizabeth on her garden path, intending to stab her with a knife secreted in his
sleeve; he had lost his nerve at the critical moment. Parry declared that he had been
playacting, trying to ensnare a real assassin, but his disclaimer did not save him.

For would-be murderers like Parry, Mary Stuart offered an alternative government. Neither Elizabeth, her courtiers, nor the realm would be safe while the
Queen of Scots lived. Assassination threatened not only the queen's life but the
people's peace. Parliament therefore enacted a law, the Act of Association, to discourage plots either by Mary herself or in her behalf. The act required Elizabeth's subjects to defend her to the death and refuse to serve any successor "by
whom and for whom" an attack had been launched. If any attempt were made
on Elizabeth's life, Mary could never be queen and indeed would die.

At last, in 1586, Francis Walsingham's men laid a trap for the Queen of Scots. They might persuade Elizabeth only by revealing Mary unmistakably as a party to an assassination plot; they must catch her in the act. Walsingham moved Mary to a house where she could be more closely controlled and appointed a new jailer less sympathetic to her than the old. Soon Mary's taste for intrigue led her into the web. She was receiving news from Europe in waterproof packages that had been inserted through the bungholes of beer kegs, put there by a double agent paid by Mary but controlled by Walsingham. Letters that the French ambassador had smuggled into England in diplomatic pouches and sent in the kegs were deciphered and read by the English government before Mary ever saw them. And Walsingham read every message from her to the outside world.

Sir Francis Walsingham, William Cecil's stern Puritan successor as secretary of state, laid a fatal trap for Mary, Queen of Scots. NATIONAL PORTRAIT GALLERY, LONDON.

The tireless Mary, a persistent bulldog in her own cause, was not satisfied with exchanging news. Walsingham intercepted letters from a network of plotters, led by a rich and idealistic Catholic squire, Anthony Babington. Sixty thousand Spanish soldiers were ready to rescue Mary, he said, and an equal number of Englishmen would rise to join them. She approved the plot in writing. Unlike the cautious Elizabeth, who had never put a word on paper during the Wyatt conspiracy, Mary now had proven her treachery in black ink. After protecting her for nineteen years, Elizabeth was forced by law to call Mary to trial before a hostile tribunal. The Queen of Scots had assured her own death.

Mary was taken with twenty-six carts of luggage to Fotheringhay Castle, a place so grim that Catherine of Aragon had refused to go there unless, as she said, she were bound and dragged. Mary's driver was dismissed, an act that ominously suggested that she would not need to travel anymore. Suffering from arthritis and weak from lack of exercise, she could no longer walk without support. Very pale, she hobbled into the trial chamber with her servants' help and was led, not to the red throne where she expected to sit, but to a crimson velvet chair. She sputtered her anger at the slight.

The outcome of the trial was set before it began. Unfamiliar with English law and still not comfortably fluent in the English language, Mary was allowed no notes, no papers, and no lawyer to defend her; as was customary in treason trials, she had to defend herself. Her accusers did not face her; their depositions were read in their absence, and she had not been permitted to see the government's evidence and plan her defense. Dissatisfied with the proof of Mary's own letter, Walsingham had forged a postscript that exaggerated her guilt.

The Queen of Scots declared her innocence and reminded her judges that anointed queens answered only to God. She had come into England trusting Elizabeth's repeated promises to assist her, but had been imprisoned instead. She asked to appear before Parliament and to meet Elizabeth, a request that recalled

Elizabeth's own desperate letter to her sister before she was sent to the Tower.

The two queens would never meet. Denied her wishes, Mary tried to charm the commission. She had not meant to topple Elizabeth, but only to maintain her place in the line of succession. Indeed, she said, she was too old and sick, too out of touch with the world, ever to occupy a throne again. She wanted only two things, freedom and the restoration of true (Catholic) religion in England. Faced with overwhelming evidence, she remained haughty. The commissioners had no more authority over her, she said, than a highwayman has over a magistrate he meets in a woods. She could not save herself, she saw; therefore she chose the role of martyr for her religion.

Mary was duly convicted and sentenced to the axe. Her jailer pulled down the overhead canopy that symbolized her royalty, and he insulted her by sitting in her presence without removing his cap. She hung a cross in the place of the royal cloth.

And yet Elizabeth dithered, still deaf to the Scottish radical John Knox's warning long ago that "if ye strike not at the root, the branches that appear to be broken will bud again." What would Mary's brother-in-law, the French king, do if Mary were destroyed? What action would King Philip of Spain and the pope take against England? How would Mary's son, James, react when he heard that England had killed his mother?

In 1572 Elizabeth had recognized the six-year-old James Stuart as King of Scots. Recently she had intercepted a letter in which Mary disinherited her twenty-year-old Protestant son and granted such rights and powers as remained hers to the Catholic King Philip. Elizabeth had sent this letter to James. Now her councilors assured her that he cared less for the mother he had scarcely known than for the throne of England. As for the Catholic monarchs, with Mary gone, they would have to rethink their entire strategy.

Still Elizabeth refused to sign the death warrant. Perhaps Mary's jailer would secretly poison her or smother her with a pillow. The suggestion offended the upstanding Puritan jailer, who refused to "make so foul a shipwreck of my conscience as to shed blood without law or warrant." Elizabeth scorned him for his "daintiness" and cursed "the niceness of those precise fellows who in words would do great things but in deed perform nothing." But she could hesitate no more.

She wrote Mary's son, James, calling his mother "the serpent that poisons me." Saving Mary would destroy Elizabeth herself. At last she angrily signed the death warrant and threw it down, directing her secretary to have it sealed and recorded. Before she could change her mind, her councilors rushed it to Fotheringhay Castle, where Mary, now forty-four years old, awaited Elizabeth's decision.

The Queen of Scots's jailers informed her that she would die in the morning. Mary had already written her farewell letters. The one to King Philip asked that he pay her servants' wages and other debts; she had always been warmly loyal to her friends. Now she lay awake all night, fully clothed, listening to the carpenters nail together the scaffold. She asked one of her ladies to read a bible story about a great sinner. After hearing the story of the good thief who died beside Jesus, Mary remarked, "In truth he was a great sinner, but not so great as I have been."

The following morning, February 8, 1587, she was brought to the Great Hall at Fotheringhay. The dining tables and chairs had been removed and a platform two feet high and twelve feet square erected in the center of the room, across from a hearth where a fire roared. On this scaffold stood a black-draped wooden block. An audience of dignitaries and local villagers had assembled to witness the execution.

Mary arrived late, walking with regal dignity and dressed like a queen in a black velvet cloak over a black silk dress with jet buttons shaped like acorns and slashed sleeves that revealed purple beneath. The white veil that covered her beautiful chestnut hair swept behind her to the floor. Two rosaries hung at her waist, and she carried a crucifix and a prayer book.

Mary's jailers had refused at first to permit her servants to accompany her. She reminded the guards that she was a Queen of France, the anointed Queen of

Scots since infancy, and, like Elizabeth herself, directly descended from England's Henry VII. Surely Elizabeth, a lone woman, would not require that Mary die alone. Her servants, she promised, would not interfere. The jailers relented and permitted Mary's two dearest women, those who slept with her in her bed, and four of her men to accompany her.

Mary sat quietly while the warrant was read. A Protestant churchman offered to pray with her and instruct her in his faith. "I am settled in the ancient Catholic Roman religion," she replied, "and mind to spend my blood in defense of it."

The cleric went on with his oral prayers anyway. Mary knelt and read Latin aloud from her own prayer book, drowning out the minister's voice. When he was quiet, she prayed in English for her son, James, for the Catholic Church, even for Elizabeth in the hope that she might serve God in the future. Mary asked God to turn his wrath away from England and begged the saints' intercession for her.

The executioner, Mr. Bull, had an axe of the kind used for chopping wood. According to custom, he asked Mary's forgiveness. "I forgive you with all my heart," she said, "for now I hope you shall make an end of all my troubles." Such grooms of the chamber had never assisted her before, she said.

Her velvet cloak fell when she stood. Her ladies helped her remove her dress, revealing her silk bodice and petticoat of crimson, a dark brownish red, the Catholic Church's symbolic color of martyrdom. She comforted her weeping servants and asked them to quiet themselves. *Ne crie point pour moi,* she said; they mustn't cry at all—she had promised their discretion. Her closest friend, Jane Kennedy, kissed the scarf Mary had chosen, a white one embroidered in gold, tied it over her eyes, and wrapped it around her head like a turban. The Queen of Scots calmly knelt on a cushion at the block, saying, "In you, Lord, is my trust, let me never be confounded." She held out her arms and said several times, "Into your hands, O Lord, I commend my spirit." Her words echoed those of the crucified Jesus.

Mary, Queen of Scots kneels under the headsman's axe, holding her crucifix, while her attendants weep and pray. Outside, workmen stoke a bonfire to destroy her clothing, the block, and all other objects stained by her blood, to prevent the creation of martyr's relics. NATIONAL GALLERIES OF SCOTLAND.

The axe fell, striking the back of Mary's head. Her ladies screamed, and she groaned. The executioner brought down a second blow across her neck. Still a strand of flesh held. The clumsy Mr. Bull sawed at it with the blade of the axe until the head was severed. He grasped the auburn hair and held it aloft, crying, "God save the Queen!" The assembly gasped, seeing that he held in his hand only an auburn wig, while the head, with its gray hair cropped short and its lips still moving, rolled at his feet. "So perish all the Queen's enemies!" the clergyman shouted.

Perhaps Mr. Bull pulled up Mary's skirts, intending to claim her green garters according to the traditional rights of the headsman. From under her crimson petticoat crept the Skye terrier that had accompanied his mistress to her death. Some witnesses may have remembered John Knox's prophecy that dogs would someday drink Mary's blood.

The little dog sat down beside the Queen of Scots's bloody shoulders and would not be lured away.

14
KING PHILIP'S HOLY WAR

AFTER MARY'S DEATH, officials undoubtedly did everything they could to wipe out her memory. They destroyed everything that had been dampened by her blood. They burned her wig and clothing and the block itself to prevent their being cut up and distributed as martyr's souvenirs. Whimpering for his mistress, her little dog was washed. It was said that he soon pined to death.

Elizabeth heard of Mary's execution calmly when she returned from a hunt. Shortly her rage began to erupt. She accused her councilors of conspiring to send an order she had never planned to deliver. Her secretary she sent to the Tower; although the threat of death was later lifted, his career was destroyed. For months she slashed William Cecil with her tongue whenever she set eyes on him.

Perhaps her rage was a theatrical exhibition, passing the blame to others so she herself could escape the wrath of Catholic Europe. In the short term the council's optimistic assurances were borne out by events. Mary's son, James, accepted his mother's death with minimal expression of pain and outrage. Burdened with strife at home, France tended to its own business.

Spain, however, was ominously silent as it prepared to invade England in the name of God. Elizabeth had restored Protestantism in England. She had joined the Protestants against Philip in the Netherlands. Now, in executing a Catholic monarch, the Queen of England had gone too far.

King Philip had changed since the days when he was Mary Tudor's husband and Elizabeth's brother-in-law. He had arrived in England as a bridegroom in velvet and pearls and ermine, dripping opulence. He was notorious then for his licentious private life. Now, however, Philip had been widowed four times, and most of his children had died young or moved far away. As he aged, he became increasingly monkish and withdrawn. In the enormous Escorial Palace, the fortress that he built, he occupied a simple interior room that was twelve feet square; it had no windows except a peephole through which he viewed the monks praying in the chapel. Contrasted with Elizabeth's gaudy style, his taste now was austere; although he received a new suit each month, each was like the others, always black and simply cut.

Philip's religious piety had hardened and intensified with the years. A scholarly man, he had collected some forty thousand books, many dealing with religious subjects. He had also amassed 7,422 relics—bones and other body parts—said to have belonged to every saint but three. Among these holy objects were 144 heads, 306 limbs, and 12 complete bodies. When the relic keeper removed any of them from a shelf at Philip's request, "the most pious king bent down and, having removed his hat or bonnet, kissed them in my hand."

Such acts are the context for Philip's vindictive actions toward the Protestant Elizabeth. Even years before, his extreme religious ideas had moved him to a remarkable gesture for the spiritual benefit of his son, Don Carlos, who had suffered head injuries. King Philip ordered that the withered corpse of a saintly cook be placed in the bed beside his unconscious son, believing that the holiness of the dead man would bless the injured one.

Now Philip's actions in the name of religion might swamp England, for his power made that of every other empire seem paltry. He controlled 20 percent of western Europe's land after 1580 and 25 percent of its population. In addition, he governed Mexico and Peru, the Philippines, and territories in Africa and Asia.

His leadership resembled Elizabeth's in some ways. He required his advisers to present written reports, reserving final decisions for himself, without discussion. She had refined a similar system, avoiding council meetings as she became more sure of herself, and asking her councilors to advise her independently in private face-to-face interviews; doing so, she prevented their ganging up on her. Philip's more radical approach isolated him from other people. Even his secretary, who worked in the next room, was required to communicate in writing. Since the king insisted on deciding every matter, great and small, he read forty to fifty reports daily.

Two men led the Spanish military forces that would cooperate in the invasion of England. The Duke of Parma commanded the army of Flanders, which, despite bankrupting expense, still occupied the Netherlands. From there Spain threatened France, the Rhineland, and—a mere forty miles across the Channel—England. Parma had governed the Netherlands ruthlessly; while Bloody Mary Tudor had burned three hundred heretics, he had burned six thousand at the stake.

As Parma headed the army, the Duke of Medina Sidonia led the navy, which docked at Cadiz. But there was a dangerous difference. Parma was an admired strategist with extensive battle experience; Medina Sidonia lacked such a practical background.

According to his habit, Philip asked these and other leaders to submit their written plans for an invasion. The bookish king, who himself had never fought a battle, analyzed their suggestions and planned the attack. He decided that Medina Sidonia would lead an armada, a huge fleet of ships. It would rendezvous with eighteen thousand of Parma's soldiers at the straits of Dover and would defend them on their voyage across the Channel in special flat-bottomed boats. They would land on a beach in Kent, southeast of London, the same place where Roman, Saxon, and Danish invaders had come ashore in earlier centuries.

The Spanish Armada itself would carry nearly thirty thousand men. According to the plan, they would unload cannons and other arms, livestock, craftsmen, and supplies, and would march rapidly toward London to assault the center of the English government. They would invade at the height of the harvest in August, when abundant food would supply the army. The Armada might engage the English navy if necessary, but its principal role would be to protect and support the invasion.

Because of Philip's secretive ways, neither Medina Sidonia and Parma nor anyone else participated in a council of war. Had Philip permitted such a conference, they might have asked how the general and the admiral would communicate. (The sixteenth century preceded by several hundred years the development of electricity and the telegraph, telephone, radio, and other rapid means of communication.) How would the ships cope with the strong currents and unpredictable winds in the Channel? Spain had no port for supplies and sanctuary; what would the Armada do in case of storms or a powerful English attack that left them lacking munitions, food, and water?

Without a war council, nobody questioned how a vast fleet of ships in Spain could sail hundreds of miles from Lisbon across fickle seas and arrive at an appointed hour (or even an appointed week) to meet an army in the Netherlands. In the meantime, the separate forces would receive news only by couriers in fast sailboats and on horseback. King Philip merely ordered his men to obey the plan. He did not ask how his orders would be carried out, assuming that, since he was acting as God's swordsman, God would protect and provide.

When the Armada arrived off the English coast near Plymouth in late July

1588, it sailed in behalf of the Catholic religion. The pope had pledged money to be delivered as soon as the Spanish set foot on English sand. The ships bore the names of saints: the *San Marcos*, the *San Esteban*, the *San Lorenzo*. Their flags were embroidered with the Spanish royal arms along with a Virgin and a Crucifixion, crossed by the red diagonal bars that symbolized holy war. Blasphemy, gambling, and other affronts to God were strictly forbidden on the ships.

Medina Sidonia described the purpose of the mission to his men in the letter containing his orders: "The principal reason which has moved his Majesty to undertake this enterprise is his desire to serve God, and to convert to His Church many peoples and souls who are now oppressed by the heretical enemies of our holy Catholic faith." The Armada, called the Enterprise of England, was a holy crusade.

King Philip's oceangoing ships were huge but awkward. Their twenty-foot cannons were not well built, had not been tested, and had no standardized caliber to suit uniform shot. The Spanish navy had developed a strategy of close-range attack after firing cannon broadsides. They were so confident of that strategy that the cannoneers who doubled as soldiers did not even bother to reload after launching their cannonballs. Instead, they abandoned the big artillery and formed boarding parties.

The command of a Spanish ship was divided, with different leadership for the soldiers and the mariners it carried. An English veteran of the Armada battle wrote that the Spanish had "more officers in their ships than we: they have a captain for their ship, a captain for their gunners and as many captains as there are companies of soldiers. . . . This breeds a great confusion. . . . They brawl and fight, commonly, aboard their ships as if they were ashore." Since nobody was in charge of swabbing the decks, "their ships are kept foul and beastly like hog-sties and sheep-cotes in comparison with ours." Each small squad of men cooked its own food on the Spanish ships. Rations were meager and badly stored.

For years, Elizabeth's spies had kept her informed of Spanish invasion plans.

In 1587, when Philip had gathered supplies for the Armada at the port of Cadiz, she had sent Sir Francis Drake, whom the Spanish called *El Draque*, The Dragon, to raid the fleet's docks. He had burned the seasoned barrel staves. The Spanish had had to build new kegs of leaky green wood, which caused the food and water they contained to spoil.

Under Elizabeth's direction, with the advice of sailors like John Hawkins, the English had built new vessels to reinforce the fleet her brother and sister had allowed to dwindle after Henry's death. She now had thirty-four ships, among them the most nimble in the world. The English navy's strength was its ships' ability to engage in fast skirmishes in familiar waters. To take advantage of the new ships' speed, a strategy evolved that emphasized cannons rather than troops, making the ships maneuverable floating platforms for heavy guns. Success depended upon their staying far enough away from the enemy to avoid being boarded.

The ships of the English Royal Navy bore names like *Triumph* and *Disdain* and were painted bright colors. The *Revenge* was green and white; the *White Bear* red. The admiral commanding them was Charles Lord Howard of Effingham, Elizabeth's first cousin through her mother. Like Medina Sidonia, he had little practical battle experience. But he had the expert counsel of the veteran mariners Sir Francis Drake and Sir John Hawkins, counsel to which he listened.

The English also shipped under a new kind of management. Drake, the privateering seaman who had sailed around the world, had developed a system of unified leadership. One experienced captain directed the entire crew instead of dividing the command, as the Spaniards did. Noblemen and gentlemen who led Spanish ships left the backbreaking work, the "haul and draw," to the lower classes. Under Drake's command, everyone, gentleman and seaman alike, joined in. English ships were relatively clean. Cooks prepared food centrally and served generous rations, with two pounds of beef allotted to each man three days each week and big servings of fish or bacon on other days.

Sir Francis Drake in 1580. The globe he holds in his hand symbolizes his triumphant voyage around the world at a time when the world was little known in England. Known as "the queen's pirate," he interrupted Spanish shipping and brought home riches. His mastery of sailing and strategy made him one of the heroes of the English battle against the Armada. NATIONAL PORTRAIT GALLERY, LONDON.

According to legend, Drake was playing bowls on the green at Plymouth when the Armada came into view. He calmly went on with his game, knowing that the English ships would have to await the turn of the tide before they could set sail. As soon as the lookouts spotted the Armada, they signaled its arrival by lighting smoky fires in a system of tall beacons that had been erected to carry that message to London. But despite ample warning of the impending crisis, England had not organized a defense. Towns and cities had flimsy protection against bombardment. Sir Walter Raleigh thought it impossible to defend the island unless "every creek, port, and sandy bay had a powerful army in each of them to make opposition." Elizabeth had put her hope in her fleet of "many movable forts . . . good ships on the sea" rather than "trust to any intrenchment upon the shore."

Consequently, the army had not built fortifications or even assembled men and supplies for the defense of England. Elizabeth had resorted instead to her usually successful delaying tactics and negotiation. Lord Admiral Howard complained that she had been holding her sailors back, like bears tied to the stake while attacked by dogs. Mindful that the strength of the kingdom depended upon a strong economy, she persisted in her financial caution, even when her kingdom faced attack. She knew that she would have to pay for a war with her own income from her lands or call on Parliament to tax the people, both repugnant options. She also dreaded losing control, as she must if she handed England over to the army and navy. Therefore, her diplomats were still conducting peace talks with the Duke of Parma when the Armada sailed.

A standing army would have been expensive to maintain, so England did not have one. The army mustered to defend England against the Armada was neither disciplined nor well trained. Nor was it well supplied. One contingent of four thousand men went to Tilbury, the town at the mouth of the Thames where military strategists expected the invasion, without a loaf of bread or a keg of beer. Commanded by Robert Dudley, the Earl of Leicester, the entire force probably numbered only about ten thousand men and faced a Spanish army at least four times as large. Leicester complained that he was more "cook, caterer and huntsman" than general.

While soldiers gathered haphazardly in the southeast, however, Drake's canny naval strategy had prevailed. Anticipating the Armada's course, and hoping to gain the advantage of the wind, he had urged that the English meet the Spanish as far west on the southern coast as possible.

And meet them they did. When Drake had finished his game of bowls and the tide and the wind had turned favorably, the English launched fifty-odd ships and set out to "singe King Philip's beard." One hundred twenty-five Spanish vessels reached Plymouth. They sailed in a close, crescent-shaped formation, with dangerous warships at the ends and clumsier merchant ships and transports protected in the center. The English strung their vessels out in a line like a snake that sailed across the Spanish fleet, shooting and keeping their distance, then turned and shot from the other side while gun crews reloaded their cannons.

The English singled out individual warships and "pluck[ed] their feathers by little and little." They harried the Spanish all along England's south coast in this manner. Elizabeth had insisted that her navy also patrol the seas near London. As the ships from Plymouth moved up the Channel, they were joined by the rest of Lord Admiral Howard's ships and by large and small private vessels. Their 197 ships carried nearly sixteen thousand men.

Despite the bombardment, the Spanish fleet crossed the Channel and arrived with little damage at the rendezvous off the Netherlands coast a week after their arrival at Plymouth. The English had stayed too far off for their shots to penetrate the Spanish ships' hulls. The Armada anchored and awaited Parma, erroneously assuming that he had received the message that announced their arrival, and begged for supplies. Not one of the messengers arrived in time, however. Nor did Medina Sidonia learn that the Dutch Protestants had blockaded Dunkirk, the Netherlands port, to stop Parma's barges.

Parma never came. The Armada ships nestled together at anchor, with the English before them and the Flemish shallows behind. At midnight, Howard launched a surprise attack of fireships. His men loaded eight vessels with flammable materials, set their masts and rigging alight, and cut them adrift. The wind and the tide carried these "hellburners" into the Armada's heart.

Howard had not expected the fires to destroy many enemy vessels, nor did they. But he succeeded in his objective: creating terror and chaos in the night. As the flaming hulks approached, their loaded guns were ignited by the fires. The Spanish cut free their ships, each secured by two or three anchors, thus losing the equipment they would need for future moorings, and escaped. In the morning, as the Armada struggled to regroup, the English closed for the kill.

The battle lasted nine hours, with the ships close enough for sailors to shout insults at their enemies and be heard. A steady wind drove the Armada northwest, away from the rendezvous, while the English tried to force them into the shoals. The Spanish could not adapt their close-quarters strategy to Howard's attack. Unprepared to reload their cannons and fight the kind of battle the English had launched, the Spanish did not even use up their munitions.

Wind and fog worsened. At closer range, the English cannon pierced the Spanish ships. Despite the gunfire, divers patched holes near the waterline as fast as possible, but they could not keep up with the destruction. The Spanish were fighting for God, but the English fought for their homes and families, remembering the undefended cities and knowing that, if the invaders landed, they might never be stopped. Several Spanish ships ran aground, though only one sank, and the sailors' wounds were terrible. The decks ran with blood, which the English could see flowing from the scuppers, the drainholes that allowed seawater to run off the deck.

The Armada was scattered and blown ever farther north from its intended meeting with Parma, unaware that now the English ships' munitions lockers were empty. In contrast, the wrecked Spanish ships still carried plenty of shot, as experts discovered when these ships were salvaged in the twentieth century. Had

With the help of a gale, the smaller, more maneuverable English ships (at left) and a more flexible battle strategy defeated the tight crescent formation of the Spanish Armada. NATIONAL MARITIME MUSEUM, GREENWICH.

Parma and Medina Sidonia met as planned, they might have crossed the Channel and sailed unchallenged up the Thames to London.

Knowing how close England had come to disaster, Howard was uncertain what to expect. Perhaps the Armada would attack through Scotland or Ireland. Perhaps they would sail back down the Channel and land near London after all.

Still unaware of the battle in the Channel and expecting the Spanish attack at any moment, Elizabeth rallied her troops at Tilbury. She passed through the encampment majestically dressed in white velvet and mounted on a white horse. There she made one of the great speeches of her life, one so stirring that the government quoted it to hearten the English people again when the Nazis launched devastating air attacks on them during World War II.

She had been warned not to risk treachery by appearing unprotected before her army, Elizabeth told her soldiers,

> but I assure you, I do not desire to live to distrust my faithful and lov-ing people. Let tyrants fear. I have always so behaved myself that, under God, I have placed my chiefest strength and safeguard in the loyal hearts and good will of my subjects, and therefore I am come amongst you, as you see, at this time, not for my recreation and dis-port, but being resolved in the midst and heat of the battle to live or die amongst you all, to lay down for my God and for my kingdom and for my people, my honour and my blood, even in the dust. I know I have the body of a weak and feeble woman, but I have the heart and stomach of a king, and of a king of England too, and think foul scorn that Parma or Spain or any prince of Europe should dare invade the borders of my realm, to which, rather than any dishonor shall grow by me, I myself will take up arms.

"Weak and feeble" woman indeed. The performance was worthy of Elizabeth's image as Gloriana, Good Queen Bess, and the Virgin Queen wedded to her people.

Never had Elizabeth's gift for oratory been more needed. She had turned over the fate of England to military men. Now, in this ceremonial gesture, she visibly took back control of England, defying the stereotype that statecraft and military action were men's work and not the business of women. A foreign diplomat praised her leadership in her country's dark hour, reporting that the queen had "not lost her presence of mind for a single moment, nor neglected aught that was necessary for the occasion. Her acuteness in resolving on her action, her courage in carrying it out, show her high-spirited desire of glory and her resolve to save her country and herself."

Ferocious storms further damaged the Spanish ships and drove them north, until their best alternative was to limp around the northern and western sides of Scotland, past Ireland, and back to Spain. Captains threw horses and mules overboard to lighten the load and preserve food and water for the men. Many surviving ships foundered on the rocks of Ireland. On one five-mile beach a witness counted "eleven hundred dead bodies of men, which the sea had driven upon the shore." In ships that remained afloat, the food was rotten and the water putrid. Half of the "invincible" Armada's men drowned, starved, or died of disease. Yet, as one exultant Englishman said, they had not "so much as sunk or taken one ship, bark, pinnace or cockboat of ours or even burned so much as one sheepcote of this land."

When Elizabeth heard news of the Armada's defeat, it is said, she rode her horse up the stairs of a hunting lodge in a fit of joy.

The Armada Jewel. This rare profile portrait, carved in stone to commemorate Elizabeth's triumph over the Spanish Armada, reveals the prominent nose and deep-set eyes that her idealized oil portraits minimize. VICTORIA AND ALBERT MUSEUM.

15
THE QUEEN AND HER WILD HORSE

ER COUNTRY HAVING BEEN ATTACKED by a foreign power, Elizabeth
had lost her claim to keeping the peace for England. Her government was impoverished despite the gradual sale of her lands. And her troubles had not ended.

In 1585 Leicester had again betrayed the queen's trust. Along with money and
seven thousand English troops, she had sent him to the Netherlands to aid the
Protestants against King Philip. He had abused his power there; against her
explicit orders, he had accepted the title of governor. Elizabeth reviled him in an
outburst that echoed King Henry's threat to her mother: Elizabeth had made
Leicester, and she could cast him down as low as she had brought him high.
There would be but one mistress in the realm, she said, and no master.

Now he had redeemed himself by organizing the chaos at Tilbury. After the
Armada victory, he enjoyed Elizabeth's favor once again, sometimes dining alone
with her, a rare privilege. Suffering stomach pain, exhaustion, and fever, however, he decided early in September 1588 to take a holiday from court.

He rested at the place where Elizabeth had stayed when she was twenty on her journey from the Tower to Woodstock. A letter he wrote there, thanking her for medicine she had given him and inquiring about her health, was the last word she ever heard from her lifelong friend. By morning he was dead, at the age of fifty-five. Some say he died of stomach cancer; others think the cause was malaria.

Elizabeth's grief did not overcome her concern for her practical advantage. She seized Leicester's great estate at Kenilworth and other lands and forced his "she-wolf" widow to sell property to pay Sweet Robin's debts to the queen. Yet Elizabeth wrote "His last letter" on the message he sent the night he died; until her own death she kept it with her most precious belongings in a pearl-covered box at her bedside.

Death made other claims on Elizabeth's circle. Walsingham died in 1590, deeply in debt despite all his godliness and hard work. Another of Elizabeth's closest friends, Christopher Hatton, who had devoted himself so exclusively to his queen that he never married, followed Walsingham to the grave; he, too, owed her a huge amount of money.

Kate Ashley and Blanche Parry, the foster mothers who had nurtured and shielded Elizabeth from infancy, were gone, and her other ladies were dying, one by one. In 1598 King Philip II of Spain would die as well. The same year, William Cecil, after being carried about the court in a chair for some time because he was unable to walk, went to bed and could not get up. The sixty-five-year-old Elizabeth visited him and fed the old man soup with her own hand. Cecil told his son that, though she would not be a mother, the queen had proven herself a most careful nurse. The mention of her loyal friend's name ever after brought tears to her eyes.

Despite her courtiers' worries about her delicate health and feminine weakness, Elizabeth had outlived most of her servants, male and female alike. Robert Cecil, William's clever, crooked-backed son, who entered Parliament at the age of eighteen, now came to prominence. The queen appointed him secretary of state, like his father. Robert Cecil was a colorless man, but color was supplied in plenty by others.

Elizabeth's courtiers matched the ostentation of her surroundings with the flamboyance of their personalities. Sir Walter Raleigh, who established Roanoke Colony and laid his magnificent cloak down in the mud to protect the queen's shoes, once attacked a man in a tavern. Raleigh filled the man's mouth with wax and tied his beard and mustache together. The very vigor that made him unreliable also attracted Elizabeth, who always liked handsome men like Raleigh.

Even more appealing than his looks was Raleigh's quick wit and sharp tongue. Elizabeth called him Water, perhaps because she could never quite get him in her grip. Once he tricked her, betting that he was so great a tobacco expert, he could determine the weight of smoke. He weighed a pipe of tobacco, smoked it, and weighed the ashes. The difference, Raleigh said, was the weight of the smoke. The queen paid up, remarking that she had heard of men who turned gold into smoke, but he was the first who turned smoke into gold.

Though Raleigh never became a trusted councilor, Elizabeth rewarded him for amusing her by making him the Captain of the Guard and giving him a profitable monopoly of licenses to sell wine. Charming though he was, he cared for nothing but his own interests, like many another courtier in Elizabeth's last years.

"When will you cease to be a beggar, Raleigh?" the queen once asked, impatient with his greed.

"When you cease to be a benefactor," he said.

Eventually, after her death, he was executed for treason.

An era in which the ears of wrongdoers were nailed to the stocks and iron yokes were locked around the necks of scolding women evoked other exaggerated actions as well. Ben Jonson, a playwright, killed an actor in a duel. Another great poet and dramatist, Christopher Marlowe, was killed at the age of twenty-eight by a stab wound above the eye. According to the official story, he was murdered by three low characters in a tavern brawl. Like Marlowe himself, however, the killers spied for Walsingham's secret service. The murder may have been a political act.

Elizabeth herself continued to enjoy her reputation for naughtiness, if not wickedness. A French ambassador who presented himself to the queen in 1597 wrote a detailed report home about the teasing exhibition she put on. She received the ambassador in her privy chamber, surrounded by courtiers and wearing a dressing gown of white taffeta lined with scarlet that exposed "the whole of her bosom." She had been ill, she said in apology for her appearance, but she fidgeted and paced up and down, as if she could not contain her energy, complaining that she was too hot.

The ambassador described the bejeweled dark-red wig she wore, with fat curls hanging down like sausages to her gem-encrusted collar, and her long, thin face with beaked nose and sunken eyes. He reported her snaggle-toothed mouth, with great gaps between uneven rotted and yellow teeth that made her words hard to understand. But he also mentioned her grace of movement, despite her sixty-four years, and the delicate whiteness of her torso. As the queen and the ambassador talked, Elizabeth ordered servants to pour water on the blazing logs in the fireplace, which raised a hissing cloud of steam.

On another occasion, the ambassador found her dressed in a gown of black and gold over white damask, a garment that fastened in the front. She flapped the edges of her dress open and shut repeatedly, "so that all her belly could be seen." Perhaps she was flirting or oblivious. Naughty as she was, though, she may have intended to make the inexperienced diplomat squirm. Her behavior then and always kept her startled visitors off balance.

The queen continued to govern imperiously. Her hearing and vision and mind were still sharp. The ambassador she entertained in the seminude thought her nevertheless a "very great Princess who knows everything." She was well informed about England and all the rest of Europe. Another ambassador, astonished by her brilliant summary of international affairs, wrote, "This great

Queen merited the whole of that great reputation she had throughout Europe."

She could still charm a diplomat with conversation to delay discussions of real issues. But her actions were sometimes grotesque. Fearful in her own palace, she kept a sword at her side. Her godson John Harington wrote, "She walks much in her privy chamber, and stamps with her feet at ill news, and thrusts her rusty sword at times into the arras [tapestry] in great rage."

As a new generation took its place in the world and the old generation died, fewer and fewer of Elizabeth's advisers remembered the vigor of her youth. They came to see her increasingly as ridiculous. One of these young men was a selfish favorite who was even more rash than Raleigh and more arrogant than his own stepfather, the Earl of Leicester. The handsome Robert Devereux, the Earl of Essex, had married Walsingham's daughter; such intermarriage was customary at court. Essex was more than thirty years younger than the queen, yet she flirted with him and kept him nearby to amuse her.

Essex had always been headstrong. Introduced to Elizabeth as a boy, he had insulted her by eluding her hand and refusing to greet her. Now one of his best friends saw him as "a man of a nature not to be ruled," excessive in his pride. He was unwilling to act the part of the queen's pet dog that Leicester had played.

Elizabeth's nickname for Essex was her Wild Horse, and she said that "someone should take him down and [teach] him better manners." Though they played cards late into the night, and people said that "he cometh not to his own lodging till the birds sing in the morning," he and the queen were continually at odds. He was "a great resenter," it was said, who "always carried on his brow either love or hatred and did not understand concealment."

In his open emotion, Essex differed from his stepfather, Leicester, who "put all his passion in his pocket." Essex always tried to wangle influential positions for his friends in order to extend his power. Once, in the council, Elizabeth refused to appoint the man Essex favored for a mission; he turned his back to

Robert Devereux, Earl of Essex, the queen's favorite, dressed in ceremonial regalia in 1597. He was so high-spirited that Elizabeth called him her Wild Horse. NATIONAL PORTRAIT GALLERY, LONDON.

her in a shocking gesture of contempt. She slapped him and told him to "get him gone and be hanged."

The Earl of Essex did not swallow such public insults with the restraint that old Cecil, Walsingham, and Leicester had found in their hearts. Shouting that he would not have accepted such treatment from even King Henry VIII, Essex went for his sword. His friends restrained him. He stormed out of the palace and fled to his own house. No one who had suggested violence against Henry would have lasted long, but Elizabeth took no immediate revenge.

Ignoring the advice of friends, Essex refused to humble himself with even a show of remorse. "What! Cannot princes err? Cannot subjects receive wrong? Is an earthly power or authority infinite? Pardon me, pardon me, my good Lord; I can never subscribe to these principles."

Nobody needed to remind Elizabeth of her inadequacies. She knew that she might be wrong, thus her indecision, but she would not have her inferiors question her judgment. Essex was doing the unthinkable, publicly doubting his monarch's perfection as God's representative, the very basis of her power. Long before democratic principles would change the world, his insolence implied that a citizen might rightly judge his leaders and their decisions. He did not speak from high-minded principles of political justice, Lacey Baldwin Smith notes; he would never have tolerated servants' challenges to his own authority. Rather he was an arrogant man, forced to obey an old woman he considered his "natural inferior" even though she was a queen.

Essex wanted adventure, fame, and power. His belligerency had caused William Cecil to refer him to Psalm 55: "Blood-thirsty and deceitful men shall not live out half their days." Essex had also proven disobedient and foolish in command of soldiers sent to reinforce the French in their war against Spain. There he neglected his mission, wasted the queen's money, and went calling like a visiting prince. Dressed like his entourage in orange velvet, he played a game of leapfrog with the French king.

In 1599 Elizabeth sent her maddening companion on a military expedition to Ireland, which even then was a diplomatic and economic swamp from which England could not extract itself. Once more Essex disobeyed the queen's orders. His rash judgment revealed itself again in negotiations with a leader of Irish rebels, talks that looked like treason. Elizabeth ordered Essex to stay in Ireland, but he returned to London anyway, while King James of Scotland sent envoys in his support.

After galloping across England to Nonsuch Palace, Essex stormed into Elizabeth's bedchamber in muddy boots, his clothing still filthy from the dash on horseback. The surprised queen sat at her dressing table, her face unadorned, her thin gray hair unwigged, her age undisguised by distractions of velvet, embroidered silk, gigantic skirts, and ropes of pearls. Essex had not only disobeyed her. Now he had embarrassed her as well.

Elizabeth would break the Wild Horse and "pull down his great heart." She relieved him of his official duties, deprived him of his profitable licenses, and had him tried for misconduct. Essex would acknowledge no error. The council committed him to house arrest. After several months, though she still banished him from court, the queen released him.

Like the temperamental Queen of Scots, however, Essex would not leave well enough alone. He wrote Elizabeth letters in the oily, flattering language of the courtly love tradition: "Till I may appear in your gracious presence, time itself is a perpetual night and the whole world a sepulcher unto your Majesty's humblest vassal." In private, he sang a different tune. Elizabeth heard a report of his rant that the queen's mind and heart were "as crooked as her carcase." He welcomed people who had grudges against her and entertained them in his house.

In 1601 Essex decided to stir the anger of a people who had been through a difficult decade: Terrible weather had spoiled the crops for several consecutive years, and food was short, misery long. Backed by hundreds of men with drawn swords, he walked through the streets of London to raise a revolution, shouting,

Robert Devereux, Earl of Essex, beheaded. Elizabeth's rebellious courtier was executed after he plotted against the queen, his benefactor. FOLGER SHAKE-SPEARE LIBRARY.

"For the Queen! For the Queen! A plot is laid for my life!" He intended to seize the court and force Elizabeth to dismiss his enemies.

The people had been enthusiastic for what they took as his heroism, but he overestimated his own popularity and the queen's weakness. A friend later said that not one citizen of London took up arms and joined him and his men. At the age of thirty-three the Earl of Essex was found guilty of treason and sentenced to death. He was cool about his execution; he "owed God a death," he said, echoing the second part of Shakespeare's recent play *Henry IV*. Two weeks later the queen was playing the virginals, surrounded by her courtiers, when a messenger arrived who knelt and announced that Essex had been beheaded on the same Tower green where Anne Boleyn had died. In the hush that followed, nobody moved. Then the music resumed as Elizabeth began to play again.

Essex was not forgotten, though. The queen spoke of him with tears in her eyes, but she said, "I warned him that he should not touch my scepter. . . . Those who touch the scepters of princes deserve no pity." Time passed, but still she said, though she had loved him, "Yet when the welfare of my state was concerned, I dared not indulge my own inclinations."

16
"THE CASE IS ALTERED"

By 1601 THE ENGLISH ECONOMY proved that Elizabeth had been right to resist war and keep a firm grip on her purse. If it was not precisely true that money was power, surely power did require money. War in Ireland, the Netherlands, and France; the Armada campaign; and the maintenance of a strong navy to ward off another possible attack from Spain had emptied the treasury. Although the people earned about the same income as they had a hundred years earlier, food cost three times as much. Inflation had also lowered the value of savings.

The need for money was so great that the queen sold to her own subjects lands worth 800,000 pounds, one fourth of her inheritance from her father. Henry's heirlooms that lay in the royal Jewel House she also put up for sale—gold chains, his great seal, two pairs of spectacles, and his gold admiral's whistle. Even such desperate measures were not enough. Elizabeth summoned Parliament and asked them to raise revenues.

The queen's frailty became gradually more apparent. She ordered the removal of mirrors from the palace to avoid the pain of seeing her aged face. At the opening of Parliament she could hardly support her heavy ceremonial robes of ermine, gold, and velvet; she staggered on the steps to the throne and was saved from a fall when the nearest nobleman caught her. But her brilliant mind had not failed her. Sensing the people's discontent, she abolished licenses and taxes that had made life for the common people hard to bear.

Once again she made a great speech: "Though God hath raised me high, yet this I count the glory of my Crown, that I have reigned with your loves." She gave her people a glimpse of her difficulties: "To be a King and wear a crown is a thing more glorious to them that see it, than it is pleasant to them that bear it." And she made a sort of promise to them: "There will never Queen sit in my seat with more zeal to my country, care for my subjects, and that will sooner with willingness venture her life for your good and safety, than myself. For it is my desire to live nor reign no longer than my life and reign shall be for your good."

She reminded them of what she had been to them and asked them to compare her with what the future might bring: "Though you have had and may have Princes more mighty and wise sitting in this seat, yet you never had nor shall have any that will be more careful and loving." At the end of the speech, she invited the gentlemen to come one by one and kiss her hand.

"We loved her," said one of her godsons, "for she said that she did love us."

Elizabeth's prodigious energy still surged and revitalized her. Her doctors begged her to abandon heavy exercise, fearing that it would kill her when old age had not. She growled and went on doing as she pleased, outliving several of those very physicians. Once she was seen through a window, dancing alone in the presence of only one lady and two musicians.

At the age of sixty-seven she still wore out her worried companions on a hunt and killed a stag with a heavy crossbow. She still walked briskly in her gardens and rode horseback, but she had to dismount and rub away the numbness in her legs. Refusing help when she boarded her barge, she lost her balance and injured her shin. She asked for a walking stick to steady herself when she climbed the stairs. Visiting a courtier's house, she complained that the walk through the many rooms exhausted her.

As Elizabeth's body failed her, ceremony propped her up. The extravagance of royal customs is implied in a description of the elaborate ritual that accompanied even an ordinary activity. After the table had been solemnly set by servants who knelt or lay facedown on the floor when they entered and left the room, as if the queen had been present, a procession of guardsmen carried in twenty-four different dishes served in gold-plated silver. Each man tasted a bite of the food he carried, to guard against the poisoning of the queen.

To the music of twelve trumpets and two kettledrums, a foreign observer noted, her ladies "lifted the meat off the table, and conveyed it into the Queen's inner and most private chamber, where, after she had chosen for herself, the rest goes to the Ladies of the Court. The Queen dines and sups alone, with very few attendants; and it is very seldom that anybody, foreigner or native, is admitted at that time." Such mechanics of power may have provided the illusion that Gloriana, the goddess, could fend off time, but death was waiting.

Elizabeth had succeeded in the career she had chosen, at a time when careers were forbidden to women. The little second-rate kingdom that she inherited had grown into a respectable power, and its reviled queen had gained the esteem of the mighty. One of the popes even said that, had she been a Catholic (and had he been free to marry, one supposes), the two would have made a great match.

Elizabeth's religious compromise had avoided the bloodbath that washed Europe. At the turn of the century her people were unified as they had never been before. They no longer considered themselves citizens of little fiefdoms run by local earls, as people had in the Middle Ages. Now they saw themselves more and more as one English people. Together they had turned back the Spanish Armada that would have changed England's history utterly.

Despite a renewed epidemic of bubonic plague that in 1603 killed thirty-eight thousand Londoners, a third of the city, the population of England had grown to 4 or 5 million. (Different historians cite various numbers.) Elizabeth had borne most war costs herself, thus keeping taxes low. A growing class of merchants, tradesmen, and craftsmen had emerged during the years of peace, comfortable people who were thriving between the impoverished peasants and the immensely rich aristocrats. Hoping for profit, these middle-class merchants financed adventurers who were exploring the world that had always been there, but that seemed a New World to a people who were only beginning to leave home.

Perhaps her greatest triumph was Elizabeth's own survival. She managed to outlive her generation and reign for nearly forty-five years. Despite the echoing loneliness of her position, she had resisted the temptation to marry, knowing that thereby she would lose her kingdom. She had kept her power despite friends who condescended to her and enemies who wished her dead. Yet Elizabeth was losing the struggle with time.

James VI, King of Scots, now received visits from Elizabeth's courtiers, as she herself had from Mary Tudor's court when Mary lay dying. The courtiers carried letters expressing hope that James would remember men loyal to him when the change of government came. Robert Cecil, looking to his future and that of England, discreetly wrote the king, hoping to assure a smooth transition and offering his own services. Like a prince forced to wait into middle age for his parents to die before ascending the throne, the young men of the court were impatient for their turn.

Elizabeth took it as a bad omen when her fingers became so swollen that the coronation ring she had worn since she was twenty-five years old had to be cut off. She was determined to defy death as intensely as she had defied her enemies and loved life. Knowing that spies carried the news of her every mishap and groan to all the thrones of Europe, she put on a brave show. Once when a downpour had made the roads impassable, she insisted on riding to her palace in London from Hampton Court, some distance away. The ride did not look promising, since she was "scarce able to sit upright."

A young courtier had the gall to advise her. "It is not meet for one of your majesty's years to ride in such a storm."

"My years!" she snorted, glowering at the nobleman. "Maids, to your horses quickly," she called, and galloped them into town to prove the courtier wrong.

Elizabeth made it a point to appear at every ceremonial function, to display her vigor to the people as visibly as possible. She was not as old as her critics thought, she insisted, as she exhibited herself in the splendor of her jewel-covered coach, drawn by horses with orange-dyed manes and tails.

Nevertheless, it was a fact that by 1603 she was becoming forgetful and her eyesight was failing. Her strong handwriting was shaky. She had lost her meager appetite and her ability to sleep soundly, and the death of a close woman friend weighed on her heart. In January, at the age of sixty-nine, Queen Elizabeth caught cold. In February she was weaker, but refused to take the medicines her doctors ordered. She paced her rooms with a fever and sore throat, unable to sleep or quench her thirst. Too weak at last to walk, she lay down on cushions arranged on the floor and refused to budge.

"Madame, to content the people you must go to bed," Robert Cecil pleaded.

"Little man, little man," she replied, "the word *must* is not to be used to princes. If your father had lived ye durst not have said so much."

Although she was unable to focus her attention on state documents, she enjoyed being read Chaucer's *Canterbury Tales,* the ladies of her bedchamber reported. Reminded of her courage by the lord admiral, who visited and persuaded her to take a little soup, she sighed and shook her head. "I am tied with a chain of iron about my neck. I am tied, I am tied, and the case is altered with me." Her famous energy had vanished, and she had lost the will to carry on.

In the first days of March, she who had always talked incessantly was silent for hours at a time. She was meditating, she told her physicians. For days Gloriana the magnificent kept her fingers in her mouth, her clothes unchanged, as she lay propped up on pillows and staring into space, eating nothing, sleeping only fitfully. At last she could no longer resist her servants. They put her gently to bed under her coverlet of gold cloth lined in ermine, guarded by the creatures carved in the wood of the bed's frame. The room was crowded with watchers, but she refused to look at them.

The privy council came to the queen's chamber at Richmond Royal Palace to speak of the succession. Should James VI of Scotland, Mary Stuart's son, follow her to the throne? Historical accounts differ: Perhaps she refused to the end to name a successor; perhaps she made a sign that she agreed. Then she asked for the archbishop. He knelt by her bedside and prayed for her soul; when he stood to go, she gestured with her hand for him to stay and go on praying. Elizabeth fell unconscious in the evening. Early in the morning of March 24, 1603, her head resting on her right arm, she died.

A waiting horseman named Carey galloped off north to Scotland. Several days later he arrived with the message to the King of Scots, who would shortly ascend the throne as James I of England. In Westminster Abbey, in the chapel of Henry VII, Elizabeth's grandfather and Mary Stuart's great-grandfather, he would erect one monument to Elizabeth Tudor and another to his mother, Mary. Henceforward, all the monarchs of England through the twentieth century would be descended from Mary Stuart, the deposed Queen of Scots. The woman who held her captive died without a blood heir.

Yet the sixteenth century has never been known for Mary Stuart, or even King Henry VIII. It is primarily the accomplishments of the great Elizabeth Tudor—Gloriana, Good Queen Bess, the maiden queen who married England—that we remember. And we honor her name by giving it to the Elizabethan Age that was in large part her creation.

Seen here from above, this marble effigy of Elizabeth I, Queen of England, tops her tomb at Westminster Abbey. To this day the bones of her half-sister, Mary I, lie in the darkness of her sepulcher, without a monument. MALCOLM CROWTHERS.

CHRONOLOGY

1491   Birth of Henry VIII.

Death of William Caxton, who introduced the printing press to England.

1492   Columbus voyages to America.

1509   Accession of Henry VIII.

Marriage of Henry VIII to Catherine of Aragon.

1516   Birth of Mary Tudor.

1527   Henry VIII begins annulment proceedings against Catherine of Aragon.

1531   Henry VIII separates from Catherine of Aragon.

1533   Henry VIII marries Anne Boleyn, then has marriage to Catherine annulled.

Birth of Elizabeth Tudor.

1536   Death of Catherine of Aragon.

Anne Boleyn executed.

Henry marries Jane Seymour.

Dissolution of monasteries.

1537   Birth of Edward Tudor.

Death of Edward's mother, Jane Seymour.

English translation of the Bible (Protestant book) published.

1540   Henry VIII marries and divorces Anne of Cleves, marries Katherine Howard.

1542   Katherine Howard executed.

Mary, Queen of Scots, born and crowned.

1543   Henry VIII marries Katherine Parr.

Reading of English Bible severely restricted.

1546   Protestants burned.

Henry suppresses Catholic councilors.

1547   Death of Henry VIII.

Accession of Edward VI.

Katherine Parr marries Thomas Seymour.

1548   Roger Ascham becomes Elizabeth's tutor.

Death of Katherine Parr.

1549   First Book of Common Prayer institutes religious ritual that replaces Catholic Mass.

John Dudley overthrows Edward Seymour.

1553   Guilford Dudley marries Jane Grey in May.

Edward VI dies in July.

Jane Grey queen for nine days.

Accession of Mary I.

1554   Sir Thomas Wyatt's rebellion ends eighteen days after it begins.

Jane Grey executed.

Elizabeth imprisoned in Tower in March; released to house arrest at Woodstock in May.

Mary Tudor marries Philip of Spain in July.

1555   Burning of Protestants begins in earnest.

Elizabeth commanded back to court.

Mary's false pregnancy.

1558   France captures Calais.

Death of Mary I.

Accession of Elizabeth I.

Marriage of Scottish Mary to Francis, heir to French throne.

1559   Elizabeth crowned.

First Parliament's religious settlement restores Protestantism as official religion.

Rumors of Elizabeth's love affair with Robert Dudley.

England assists Protestant rebels in Scotland.

Francis II and Mary, Queen of Scots, become King and Queen of France.

1560   Treaty of Edinburgh expels French from Scotland, makes it a Protestant nation.

Death of Amy Robsart, Robert Dudley's wife.

Death of King Francis II of France.

1561   Widowed Mary returns to Scotland from France, asserts her claim to throne of England.

1562   Elizabeth I nearly dies of smallpox.

1563   Soldiers home from France bring bubonic plague, which kills 17,000 in London.

Second Parliament of Elizabeth's reign, called to levy taxes, pressures her to marry or name her successor.

1564   Robert Dudley created Earl of Leicester.

Efforts to marry Leicester to Mary, Queen of Scots.

1565   Mary marries Henry Stuart, Lord Darnley.

Kate Ashley dies.

1566   Third Parliament of Elizabeth's reign uses financial pressure in attempt to secure succession.

Birth of James VI of Scotland, later James I of England.

1567   Darnley murdered.

Mary Stuart marries Earl of Bothwell, Darnley's suspected assassin.

Mary deposed, imprisoned in Scotland.

1568   Mary flees to England.

Duke of Norfolk and Mary conspire to marry.

1569   Northern Catholic rebellion against Elizabeth's regime.

1569–72 Rising hostility between England and Spain.

1569–87 John Hawkins refits English navy, preparing for attack.

1570   Pope excommunicates Elizabeth. Ridolfi plot begins.

1571   Duke of Norfolk implicated in Ridolfi plot.

1572	William Cecil becomes lord treasurer.
1573	Francis Walsingham becomes secretary of state.
1573–76	Marriage negotiations between Elizabeth and Francis, Duke of Alençon (Frog).
1577–80	Francis Drake sails around the world.
1578	James VI, age twelve, succeeds to Scottish throne.
1579	Husband of Lettice Knollys dies. Sometime thereafter, Leicester secretly marries her.
1580	Jesuit missionaries illegally arrive in England.
1581	Elizabeth publicly gives ring to Alençon, abruptly decides against marriage.
1584	Parliament passes Act of Association, aimed at Mary Stuart, to punish and prevent succession of any party to conspiracy against the crown.
1585	War with Spain in the Netherlands.
1586	Trial of Mary Stuart.
1587	Mary Stuart executed.
	Drake attacks Armada moored at Cadiz.
1588	Armada launches attack on England in late July, defeated by English navy.
	Elizabeth addresses English army at Tilbury August 8.
	Leicester dies in November.
1590	Death of Walsingham.
1592	First performance of a play by William Shakespeare.
1594–97	Poor harvests, rise in food prices.
1594–1603	Rebellion in Ireland.
1598	Deaths of William Cecil and King Philip II of Spain.
1601	Robert Devereux, Earl of Essex, executed.
1603	Elizabeth I dies of abscessed throat.
	Accession of James VI of Scotland as James I of England.
	Thirty-eight thousand Londoners die of plague.

BIBLIOGRAPHY AND SOURCE NOTES

OVERALL

Dozens of biographies and histories of Elizabeth Tudor and her age contributed facts, personal details, and historical interpretations to this work. In the following partial list of sources, arranged by chapter, readers may explore particular topics further.

Three books were especially useful because of their thoroughness, sprightly prose, vivid detail, or original approach and ideas. Even when they were not cited directly, they informed every chapter of this new work:

Erickson, Carolly. *The First Elizabeth*. New York: Summit, 1983.

Smith, Lacey Baldwin. *The Horizon Book of the Elizabethan World*. New York: American Heritage, 1967.

————. *Elizabeth Tudor: Portrait of a Queen*. Boston: Little, Brown, 1975.

Several other useful sources provided a general context:

Elton, G. R. *England Under the Tudors*. London: Methuen, 1955.

Neale, J. E. *Queen Elizabeth*. New York: Harcourt, 1934.

Plowden, Alison. *Elizabethan England: Life in an Age of Adventure*. London: Reader's Digest, 1982.

Rowse, A. L. *The England of Elizabeth: The Structure of Society*. New York: Macmillan, 1951.

Tillyard, E. M. W. *The Elizabethan World Picture*. New York: Macmillan, 1934.

Weir, Alison. *The Children of Henry VIII*. New York: Ballantine, 1996.

SOURCES BY CHAPTER

Chapter 1. *The Midnight Crow*

Erickson, Carolly. *Mistress Anne*. New York: Summit, 1984.

Ridley, Jasper. *Henry VIII*. London: Constable, 1984.

SIXTEENTH-CENTURY IDEAS, ASSUMPTIONS

Smith. *The Horizon Book of the Elizabethan World*.

Tillyard. *The Elizabethan World Picture*.

Chapter 2. *Sisters*

ELIZABETH'S BIRTH AND CHRISTENING

Erickson. *The First Elizabeth*.

TREATMENT OF MARY TUDOR

Erickson, Carolly. *Bloody Mary: The Life of Mary Tudor*. New York: Morrow, 1978.

ANNE'S TRIAL
Warnicke, Retha M. *The Rise and Fall of Anne Boleyn: Family Politics in the Court of Henry VIII.* Cambridge, England: Cambridge University, 1989.

Chapter 3. *The Midnight Crow's Daughter*
EVERYDAY LIFE, ATTITUDES ABOUT MONARCHY
Smith. *The Horizon Book of the Elizabethan World.*

EDUCATION
Erickson. *Bloody Mary.*
————. *The First Elizabeth.*

ELIZABETH'S INFANCY, CHILDHOOD, YOUTH
Plowden, Alison. *The Young Elizabeth.* London: Macmillan, 1971.

ATTITUDES TOWARD WOMEN
Smith. *The Horizon Book of the Elizabethan World.*
————. *Elizabeth Tudor.*

Chapter 4. *The Princess and the Admiral*
ELIZABETH AND THOMAS SEYMOUR
Erickson. *The First Elizabeth.*
Plowden. *The Young Elizabeth.*

VALUE OF MONEY
Nicholl, Charles. *The Reckoning: The Murder of Christopher Marlowe.* New York: Harcourt, 1992.

Chapter 5. *Bloody Mary*
Erickson. *Bloody Mary.*
———— . *The First Elizabeth.*
Marshall, Rosalind K. *Mary I.* London: Her Majesty's Stationery Office, 1993.

Chapter 6. *Subject to Her Sister*
ELIZABETH'S IMPRISONMENT
Plowden. *The Young Elizabeth.*
Neale. *Queen Elizabeth.*

KING PHILIP OF SPAIN
Erickson. *The First Elizabeth.*
————. *Bloody Mary.*

CATHOLIC COUNTER REFORMATION
Smith. *The Horizon Book of the Elizabethan World.*

Chapter 7. *The New Queen Crowned*
CONDITION OF ENGLAND
Erickson. *The First Elizabeth.*
Rowse. *The England of Elizabeth.*

CORONATION
Erickson. *The First Elizabeth.*
Plowden. *Elizabethan England.*

Chapter 8. *The New Queen in Charge*
Jones, Norman. *The Birth of the Elizabethan Age: England in the 1560s.* Oxford: Blackwell, 1993.

ELIZABETH'S EARLY GOVERNMENT
MacCaffrey. *Elizabeth I.*
————. *The Shaping of the Elizabethan Regime: Elizabethan Politics, 1558–1572.* Princeton, NJ: Princeton University, 1968.
Smith. *Elizabeth Tudor.*

RELIGIOUS ISSUE AND RESOLUTION
Neale. *Queen Elizabeth.*
Plowden, Alison. *Danger to Elizabeth: The Catholics Under Elizabeth I.* London: Macmillan, 1973.
Smith. *The Horizon Book of the Elizabethan World.*
————. *Elizabeth Tudor.*

ANTICLERICAL THEATRICS
Erickson. *The First Elizabeth.*

EFFECTS OF RAPID CHANGE ON ENGLISH PEOPLE
Smith. *The Horizon Book of the Elizabethan World.*

Chapter 9. *"The Queen's a Woman!"*
ATTITUDES TOWARD WOMEN
Hibbert, Christopher. *The Virgin Queen: Elizabeth I, Genius of the Golden Age.* New York: Addison-Wesley, 1991.

MARRIAGE ISSUE
Plowden, Alison. *Marriage with My Kingdom: The Courtships of Elizabeth I.* New York: Stein & Day, 1977.

Chapter 10. *Sweet Robin*
Haynes, Alan. *The White Bear: The Elizabethan Earl of Leicester.* London: Peter Owen, 1987.

Jenkins, Elizabeth. *Elizabeth and Leicester.* London: Gollancz, 1961.

Osborne, June. *Entertaining Elizabeth: The Progresses and Great Houses of Her Time.* London: Bishopsgate, 1989.

Plowden. *Marriage with My Kingdom.*

Chapter 11. *The Troublesome Queen of Scots*
Erickson. *The First Elizabeth.*

Fraser, Antonia. *Mary, Queen of Scots.* London: Weidenfeld, 1969.

Sitwell, Edith. *The Queens and the Hive.* London: Macmillan, 1962.

Chapter 12. *A Very Public Private Life*
Arnold, Janet. *Queen Elizabeth's Wardrobe Unlock'd.* Leeds, England: Maney, 1988.

Hibbert, Christopher. *The English: A Social History 1066–1945.* New York: W. W. Norton, 1987.

Halliday, F. E. *An Illustrated Cultural History of England.* London: Thames and Hudson, 1967.

———. *Shakespeare and His World.* New York: Viking, 1956.

Plowden. *Elizabethan England* .

Ridley, Jasper. *The Tudor Age.* London: Constable, 1988.

Rowse, A. L. *William Shakespeare: A Biography.* New York: Harper & Row, 1963.

———. *The Elizabethan Renaissance: The Cultural Achievement.* London: Macmillan, 1972.

Strong, Roy. *The Cult of Elizabeth.* New York: Thames and Hudson, 1977.

———. *Gloriana: The Portraits of Queen Elizabeth.* London: Thames and Hudson, 1987.

ELIZABETH'S CLOTHING, HAIR AND COSMETICS
Erickson. *The First Elizabeth.*

Chapter 13. *To Kill the Queen*
Haynes, Alan. *Invisible Power: The Elizabethan Secret Services 1570–1603.* Phoenix Mill, Gloucestershire, England: Alan Sutton, 1992.

Plowden. *Danger to Elizabeth.*

Jenkins, Elizabeth. *Elizabeth the Great.* New York: Coward McCann, 1959.

MacCaffrey, Wallace T. *Queen Elizabeth and the Making of Policy, 1572–1588.* Princeton, NJ: Princeton University, 1981.

Smith, Lacey Baldwin. *Treason in Tudor England: Politics and Paranoia.* Princeton, NJ: Princeton University, 1986.

Chapter 14. *King Philip's Holy War*
MacCaffrey, Wallace T. *Elizabeth I: War and Politics 1588–1603*. Princeton, NJ: Princeton
    University, 1992.

KING PHILIP'S RELIGIOUS ATTITUDES, ENGLISH AND SPANISH STRATE-
GIES, DETAILS OF BATTLE
Martin, Colin, and Geoffrey Parker. *The Spanish Armada*. London: Hamish Hamilton, 1988.

ENGLISH EXPLORATION, SLAVE TRADE
Rowse, A.L. *The Elizabethans and America: The Trevelyan Lectures at Cambridge 1958*. London:
    Macmillan, 1959.
————. *The Expansion of Elizabethan England*. London: Macmillan, 1955.

Chapter 15. *The Queen and Her Wild Horse*
Smith. *Elizabeth Tudor*.
————. *Treason in Tudor England*.
Erickson. *The First Elizabeth*.
MacCaffrey. *Elizabeth I*.

ATTITUDES TOWARD HIERARCHY
Smith. *Elizabeth Tudor*.
————. *The Elizabethan World*.

Chapter 16. *"The Case Is Altered"*
Erickson. *The First Elizabeth*.
Williams, Neville. *The Life and Times of Elizabeth I*. London: Weidenfeld, 1972.
MacCaffrey. *Elizabeth I: War and Politics*.
Smith. *Elizabeth Tudor*.

INDEX

Page numbers in *italics* refer to illustrations or captions.